D0622993

CP 12

FAMOUS REGIMENTS

The Royal Scots

FAMOUS REGIMENTS

Edited by
Lt-General Sir Brian Horrocks

The Royal Scots
(The Royal Regiment)

by
A. Michael Brander

Leo Cooper Ltd, London

First published in Great Britain 1976
by Leo Cooper Ltd,
196 Shaftesbury Avenue,
London WC2H 8JL

Copyright © 1976 by A. Michael Brander
Introduction Copyright © 1976 by
General Sir Peter Hunt

ISBN 0 85052 183 1

Printed in Great Britain
by Clarke, Doble & Brendon Ltd,
Plymouth

Illustrations

The author and publishers would like to thank the following for permission to reproduce copyright illustrations: The Army Museums Ogilby Trust, Nos 1 and 5; The Imperial War Museum, Nos, 7, 8, 9, 10, 11, 12, and 13; *The Scotsman*, No 15

Acknowledgements

My thanks are due to the following:

The staff at the Regimental Museum at Edinburgh Castle for the use of their books and records and in particular Col D. A. D. Eakin, DSO and Col B. A. Fargus, OBE (who checked the typescript and made several helpful suggestions).

The Imperial War Museum and the Army Museums Ogilby Trust for many of the illustrations, and their staff, especially Major Dawnay, for their help in selecting those used.

Mr W. N. Willis, late 10th Hussars P.W.O., for allowing me to quote extracts from the unpublished letters of his grandfather, Private John Willis, written in the Crimea.

My father, for his help, criticism and comments, and above all for his initial suggestion.

Introduction

by General Sir Peter Hunt, GCB, DSO, OBE

I first met The Royal Scots thirty-nine years ago, in 1937. This is only a short period of time in the life of a Regiment of the Line whose history goes back 343 years, but it is a not inconsiderable slice of one's own, and it has covered some eventful years.

I remember this first occasion very clearly. I was a very junior subaltern in my Regiment, the Queen's Own Cameron Highlanders, then stationed at Catterick Camp, and together with a number of brother officers, I had been invited to the Officers' Mess of the 1st Battalion The Royal Scots to a Regimental Guest Night, shortly after their arrival in Catterick. It was, as one might expect, a happy and friendly occasion, boisterous perhaps, and definitely an evening to remember. I shall not easily forget, for instance, the firm but diplomatic way in which their Adjutant, later to become a distinguished senior Army officer and Governor of the State of Victoria in Australia, finally persuaded the younger guests that it was perhaps time to leave for home!

Ever since that evening in Yorkshire, I have been able to follow, in one way or another, and from different viewpoints, the fortunes of The Royal Scots in war and peace. The 1st Battalion joined us in the 2nd Division, at Aldershot, on their return from Palestine in early 1939, and it was only a few months later that we were all making our way to France as part of the British Expeditionary Force.

We were next-door neighbours on the French-Belgian frontier during the winter months of 1939/40, and when the so-called 'phoney war' was abruptly ended by the German invasion of the Low Countries on 10 May, 1940, we marched together into Belgium and up to the River Dyle in front of Brussels.

At that time I was Adjutant of my Battalion and we were all

actively involved in the fighting on the Dyle and during the subsequent long retreat to Dunkirk. At Calonne, on the Escaut Canal, we were alongside The Royal Scots dealing with a most determined enemy in and around that village. I was wounded there, but, thankfully as it turned out, I was able to remain with my Battalion and so was able to witness shortly afterwards and from close at hand the 1st Royal Scots' defence, against overwhelming odds, of their sector of the La Bassée Canal. Heavily engaged though we ourselves were, I remember my own 'Jocks', who must have had many friends among the ranks of the 1st Royal Scots, telling me that 'The Royal Scots always fought like this'.

The months after Dunkirk were months of reconstitution and reorganization, and I among many others was posted away from the 2nd Division and did not therefore go overseas with that Division when they left in the middle of 1942 for India and subsequently Burma and Assam. It was during 1944 that, in perhaps the fiercest battle of the Japanese war, The Royal Scots and the Camerons once again found themselves fighting side by side on the hills and in the jungles around Kohima.

Happily, I found myself, in early 1944, not very far away from another Battalion of the Regiment – the 8th. They were busy training, as part of the 15th Scottish Division, for the opening of the 'Second Front'. I saw much of them then and subsequently, both as a staff officer at Divisional Headquarters, and later as the Commanding Officer of the 7th Seaforth Highlanders in the same Division.

I have happy memories of meetings on training and at sporting occasions in Northumberland and Yorkshire before 'D' Day, and later, during the campaign itself, we advanced together up the long road from the Normandy beaches into Belgium and over the Albert Canal into the Gheel bridgehead. The magnificent fight of the 8th Royal Scots at Aart, where the battalion lost eleven officers and 207 other ranks killed, wounded and missing, was, I remember, a source of admiration and pride to the whole 15(S) Division.

Later that year, at Blerick in Holland, on the River Maas, the

8th Royal Scots took part in what later came to be known as 'the model set-piece attack' by armour and infantry against formidable minefield and wire obstacles, and dug-in positions heavily supported by artillery from the far bank of the river. For this operation, my battalion of Highlanders was temporarily under command of 44 (Lowland) Infantry Brigade, to which The Royal Scots belonged, and I remember how determined we were not to be outdone! I think honours were even; it certainly was a most successful operation in which fittingly the 8th Royal Scots were on 'the right of the line'.

We were involved together in the confused Rhineland battle, where the 8th Battalion distinguished itself particularly at Cleve and Goch; at the Rhine crossings; and finally during the advance to and crossing of the River Elbe. So the war ended, but before the 15(S) Division was disbanded, and its battalions dispersed or themselves disbanded, The Royal Scots earned one more, albeit small, feather to put in their caps – a company football team from the 8th Battalion comfortably defeated a team representing the full might of a nearby Russian battalion!

I have been fortunate in the years since the Second World War to have been able to keep in touch with The Royal Scots. As Chief of Staff Scottish Command, between 1962 and 1964, I saw much of the 8th/9th Territorial Battalion in Edinburgh and the Lothians, whose keenness and efficiency typified the Regiment. In more recent times, as a NATO Army Group Commander and as Chief of the General Staff, I have been able to visit and meet the officers and men of the 1st Battalion, carrying out their duties in UK, Northern Ireland and Cyprus, and as the British Army's representatives in the multinational Allied Command Europe Mobile Force. I was often told by my NATO colleagues how their high professional standards in this latter role were a source of admiration to all who came in contact with the battalion.

In another less obvious but no less pleasing way, I have a very happy link with the Royal Scots. For eight and a half years and until recently I was Colonel of the 10th Princess Mary's Own Gurkha Rifles, whose affiliation to The Royal Scots was formally recognized in 1950 after a friendship of nearly half a century. HM The King at that time honoured the 10th Gurkha Rifles by permitting them to bear the name of his sister, HRH Princess Mary, The Princess Royal, the much-loved Colonel-in-Chief of The Royal Scots. On the many occasions, both formal and informal, that I have had occasion to visit my Gurkhas, it was always with the greatest pleasure I saw the 'Hunting Stewart' tartan on parade, with the pipers of the Regiment, who have been trained by The Royal Scots from as far back as 1895, playing the old tunes so familiar to many thousands of 'Royals'.

Tradition, old established customs, family connections: all are part and parcel of the make-up of a Scottish Regiment. They are of priceless value and The Royal Scots, The 1st of Foot, whose history is virtually the history of the British Army, have always used these assets to the best possible advantage. However, in these difficult days of changing social values and economic strains, these are not in themselves enough.

To remain on top of one's job at a time when many people outside it seem to regard it almost as an irrelevancy, demands high professional dedication and skill, cheerful enthusiasm for the daily round, and above all, despite an era of so-called peace, a readiness to fight and perhaps give one's life for one's country. These qualities The Royal Scots have always had, and still have.

Mr A. Michael Brander, himself the son and grandson of a Royal Scot, has written an admirable short history of the Regiment, and I commend it most warmly to all those who seek to be heartened by a story of unrivalled endeavour and sacrifice over 343 years, in almost every part of the world, in the service of the Crown.

Chapter 1

THE ROYAL SCOTS, the oldest Regiment in the British Army, can trace its origins directly back to 1633 when Sir John Hepburn raised a body of men in Scotland for service in France under Louis XIII. Such foreign service by Scottish soldiers was, in itself, no new phenomenon. As early as the late ninth century Charles III of France is reputed to have had a Scottish bodyguard, and in the mid-thirteenth century a Scottish contingent fought under Louis IX in the Eighth Crusade. With the founding of the 'auld alliance' in 1295 such service became more frequent and more formalized. Many Scots fought for France in the later stages of the Hundred Years War and distinguished themselves to such an extent that the survivors were formed into the Scottish Archer Guard (*Les Gardes du Corps Ecossoises*), the bodyguard of the King of France, and later also the Scottish Men-at-Arms (*Les Gens d'Armes Ecossoises*). After the failure of the English attempt to absorb France an increasing number of Frenchmen found their way into these regiments. The Scots element was, however, augmented in the 1590s by contingents sent over to support the claims of Henry of Navarre to the throne.

Scottish troops were by no means confined to service for France. Following the outbreak of the Thirty Years War (1618) a Scottish regiment was raised in 1620 by Sir Andrew Gray to fight in Bohemia on behalf of Frederick V, the Elector Palatine, known to history as 'The Winter King'. On Frederick's defeat in the same year at the Battle of the White Mountain the regiment retired to Holland, where it continued to fight against the Spanish. In 1623 Sir Andrew Gray handed over to Sir John Hepburn, a native of Athelstaneford in East Lothian, who had commanded a company in Bohemia, and Hepburn took the regiment into the service of Gustavus Adolphus of Sweden.

Gustavus Adolphus, the 'Lion of the North', was the most advanced military commander of his day. His troops were well trained and exceptionally mobile. Under him Hepburn's regiment fought in Poland, Prussia and Pomerania between 1623 and 1630. They were not the only Scottish regiment in Swedish service. For instance a regiment under the command of Sir Donald Mackay (Lord Reay) joined the Swedes in 1629 after distinguishing itself in Danish service. On Sweden's entry into the Thirty Years War in 1630 Hepburn's Regiment, Mackay's Regiment and two other Scottish regiments, Lumsden's Musketeers and Stargate's Regiment, combined to form the Green Brigade under Hepburn's command.

By 1632 the Green Brigade was famous throughout Europe, but in that year, after a quarrel with Gustavus Adolphus, Hepburn left to serve for France, and the next year Hepburn raised his force in Scotland under the Royal Warrant. This newly recruited force was supplemented by elements of the Scottish Archer Guard and the Scottish Men-at-Arms. In 1635 the *Regiment d'Hébron*, as it was called, assumed its final form with the transfer to it of the Scottish regiments in Swedish service. Though heavily depleted in numbers, thirteen regiments in all were transferred and Hepburn now commanded a force of over 8,000 men, widely regarded as among the best in Europe.

The Regiment as now constituted contained many different units of diverse origins. However, their Commanding Officer's original force had been raised under the Royal Warrant. It is from the date of issue of the Warrant, 28 March, 1633, that the King assumed some authority over the troops raised by Sir John Hepburn. This authority extended to later additions to the original force, whatever their source, and it was by virtue of the Royal Warrant that the entire regiment under Hepburn's command, from 1633 onwards, was a British regiment. It was a regular force in a standing army which could be recalled to Britain at will.

In the meantime, however, the Regiment continued in French service. Moreover it achieved the unique distinction of being recognized as the first regiment in both England and France. The connection with the long-standing Scottish Archer Guard, when combined with the absorption of the units under Swedish service, gave the Regiment such strength and prestige that it was able to claim and obtain precedence over all others in the French service. This caused some feeling, particularly with the Regiment of Picardy, which traced its origins back to 1562, and it was the first to apply the nickname 'Pontius Pilate's Bodyguard' to the Regiment. The soubriquet was turned against the Picardy Regiment, however, by one of Hepburn's officers. In a dispute with an officer of the Picardy Regiment, referring to the well known fact that the Regiment had been caught sleeping at their posts, Hepburn's man retorted sarcastically: 'You must be mistaken, sir; for had we really been the Guards of Pontius Pilate and done duty at the sepulchre, the Holy Body had never left it.'

In 1636 Sir John Hepburn was killed at the siege of Saverne, near Strasbourg. His death aroused such anger among his troops that they stormed the supposedly impregnable castle, crushing all resistance. Hepburn was only 38 when he died, the first and one of the greatest Colonels of the Regiment. He was knighted in 1629 by Gustavus Adolphus and died a Marshal of France. Had he lived he would probably have ranked among the greatest military figures of his day. A twenty-five foot memorial erected by Louis XIV in Toul Cathedral bore witness to the respect he had won in France, and Cardinal Richelieu wrote, 'I cannot express how much I am affected by the death of poor Colonel Hepburn, not only because of the great esteem in which I held him, but also for the great zeal and devotion which he had always shown in the service of His Majesty. His loss has so pained me that I cannot be consoled.' Sir John was succeeded by his cousin George Hepburn, who was killed at Damvillers in 1637. From then until 1688 three Douglases were Colonels successively, the regimental title being altered accordingly.

During the second half of the Thirty Years War, from 1633 onwards, the Regiment saw heavy fighting. It moved up the

Rhine in 1633–4, back into Lorraine in 1635–6, and from 1639 to 1643 it was in Picardy and the North-East of France. After a brief spell in Italy in 1643 the Regiment returned to Northern France the following year, but was not heavily engaged for the last four years of the war up to 1648. The Regiment also fought on behalf of the King in the French Civil War (1649–52) and against the Spaniards in the Netherlands in the Franco-Spanish War (1655–9).

Throughout these years the Regiment's numbers were steadily declining. Recruiting was affected by the Civil War in Britain, and by the demands of other Scottish regiments serving on the continent, so that it rarely kept pace with the casualty rate, which was exacerbated by the increased use of firearms and grenades, allied to the preponderance of siege warfare. The Regiment fought in a large number of sieges between 1633 and 1648. The medieval castles had become fortresses, protected by earthworks, ditches and trenches, against which the attacker had to throw up his own system of trenches and gun emplacements, so that trench warfare probably constituted as much of the fighting as did open warfare. An eyewitness account of the siege of Breda in 1637 by Scottish troops in Dutch service gives some idea of why losses were so high in this type of fighting:

'Now with much difficulty had the Scots made a Bussebridge over the mouth of the Horneworke, where fastening a mine within the bosome of an earthen Rampier, which being blowne, it rebounded back on themselves (being the Engineer's fault), yet without any damage save only a part of the Bridge broken downe. Then was Lieutenant Gladstanes commanded by the General to fall on, and with his divers officers and some choice companies of selected souldiers, which indeed they both bravely and manfully accomplished, and with them fall on a certain number of uncommanded voluntiers, all Scotsmen. The conflict for an hour's space was exceedingly doubtful and dangerous for the Muskets and Firelocks never ceased, neither was the Sword and Pike short of the manliest usage couragious valour could afford magnanimous gallants.

'At last the enemy was beaten out of the body of the Horne-worke, and above three score of them left there killed, and retired to a cross Demilune, erected within the inmost corner of the worke, from which place they damnably threw over Handgarnads, Bullets of three pounds weight, and being empty within, they are filled with Powder, Pitch and Sulphur, where falling on the ground and breaking, spoyled a number of our men. Then came certain companies of Dutch Firelockes to second them, and gave once fire, but by your leave they left the service and fell a spoiling of the dead bodies which the Scots had slaine.'

The close of the Thirty Years War also marked the beginning of the end of the Regiment's history as a force serving foreign masters. In 1650 Charles II tried unsuccessfully to regain his father's throne, but on this occasion the French authorities required the services of the Regiment in the French Civil War and refused to let it go. So it was not until 1661, the year after the Restoration, when Charles again appealed for the Regiment to help suppress the revolt of the Fifth Monarchy Men, that it first travelled to England. The revolt of the Fifth Monarchy Men came to little, and in fact the Regiment's chief task, before it returned to France in 1662, was to bridge the gap between the disbanding of the New Model Army and the creation of the New Regular Army. The New Regular Army was organized along the same lines as the New Model Army, which it replaced, and that in turn had been evolved in imitation of the British units in foreign service. The Regiment was thus the original model of all and rightly took its place as the First Regiment of Foot in the new army.

On its return to France the Regiment did four years garrison duty before its recall to England in 1666, necessitated by Louis XIV's alliance with the Dutch against Britain. After reaching England the Regiment's strength was increased from eight companies of 100 each to twelve of 100 each, and it seems that it may have been formed into two battalions, but if so the division did not last for long. The Regiment was assigned to the defence of Chatham against the Dutch fleet and fulfilled its task despite considerable disadvantages, including apparently, the distrust of the locals, as noted by Pepys in his diary: 'Here in the streets I did hear the Scotch march beat by the drums before the soldiers, which is very odde. . . . They are far more terrible to these people of the country towns than the Dutch themselves.'

In 1667 the Regiment returned to France, now 1,500 strong, and for the first time definitely known to be wearing red coats. The coats were lined with white and reached the knees, serving as both jacket and greatcoat. They were worn over a shirt, and possibly a waistcoat, with white or light-grey knee breeches and heavy shoes and stockings. A broad-brimmed hat and a neck-cloth completed this generally practical garb, which was worn with hair long, covering the back and sides of the neck.

After another four years of garrison duty in France, in 1672 the Regiment once again went into action against the Dutch, this time on behalf of the French. It took part in several sieges and apparently encountered some of the Scottish troops serving for the Dutch. A Captain Mackully of one of these units reports of the surrender of Navagne: 'If they had not surrendered when they did, they must have lost it upon the attack, and that it was a battalion of my Lord Douglas's Regiment that were entered the Trenches to have attacked them, who first entered and took possession of the fort.'

With the signing of peace between Britain and Holland in 1674 the Regiment was withdrawn from the Dutch front and sent to serve on the Rhine against Austria. In its first probe across the Rhine to find the enemy, in the autumn of 1674, the Regiment had with it as a volunteer the commander of another British regiment who was to become one of the greatest of British generals, John Churchill, later Duke of Marlborough. The campaign was not generally popular among the British troops, for whom it held little interest, and desertions were regrettably frequent. Nonetheless the Regiment won special praise from Louis XIV for its defence of Treves, in which it was outstanding for its determination to fight on long after the rest of the garrison wanted to surrender.

Meanwhile, in Britain, there was growing opposition to Charles's policy of lending troops abroad and to his friendship with France. In 1678 this finally resulted in the recall of the Regiment, now Dumbarton's Regiment, Lord George Douglas having been created Earl of Dumbarton in 1675. The recall marked the end of an era, for the Regiment was never again to serve a foreign master. The small body of troops raised by Hepburn in 1633 was now the oldest British regiment, yet it had seen almost no service for Britain. In the years that were to follow it was to uphold for Britain the traditions of service that had been created abroad, not just since 1633, but intermittently and indirectly for many centuries before that date.

Chapter 2

IN 1680 the Regiment was posted to Tangier, its first station abroad in British service. Tangier had come to Britain as part of the dowry of Charles II's bride. It was, however, as much a liability as an asset, since it was being vigorously attacked by the Moors, determined to drive all foreigners from their coast, and the defences, as well as being overlooked by a series of hills, were in a bad state of disrepair. On the Governor's urgent request for the assistance of the Regiment, referred to variously as the Ancient Scotch, the Scotch Regiment or Dumbarton's, it moved to Tangier in detachments from Ireland, whence it had been posted in the previous year and where it left five companies. The detachments included a grenadier company, added in 1677 or '78, whose task it was to throw hand-grenades and destroy field palisades.

The first detachment arrived at a critical stage of the siege. The Moors, by means of trenches, had cut off the outworks from the main defences of the town. Two outlying forts had had to surrender and a third, Fort Charles, was so hard-pressed that the first detachment was detailed to sally forth and help the garrison back. Though this seems to have been regarded as a particularly desperate venture the detachment managed to meet up with the retiring garrison and escort them to safety, despite severe casualties.

After the arrival of the other detachments the British embarked on the offensive. The fighting consisted predominantly of trench warfare and the grenadier company appears to have been particularly active, as a notable feature was the way in which the Moors were grenaded from their positions. The Regiment bore the brunt of the struggle and captured an enemy colour as well as playing a part in the decisive defeat of the Moors towards the end of the year. A treaty was then signed and the Regiment remained in garrison during the ensuing peace, until it was withdrawn on the abandonment of Tangier in early 1684.

As a result of its efforts the Regiment was awarded 'Tangier' as its first battle honour, and on its return to England the title 'The Royal Regiment of Foot' was conferred by Charles II. For the time being the Regiment remained in garrison in the South of England, but with James II's accession and Monmouth's rebellion in 1685 five companies were detailed to accompany the force concentrated against the rebels, whom they met at Sedgemoor.

Monmouth had fought beside the Regiment in France and, on recognizing them from his vantage point in the tower of Bridgewater Church, is reputed to have said, 'I know these men will fight. If I had them, I would not doubt of success.' In the event his appreciation of their qualities was to be fully justified. Deciding that he could only win by surprise, he determined to make a night attack. The officers of the Royal Regiment, however, dissatisfied with the general defence arrangements, had taken special precautions of their own. Consequently, when Monmouth attacked, the Royal Regiment stood to arms at once, giving the other troops time to form and repulse the attack. The rebels were then easily defeated, Monmouth's standard being captured by Captain Hackett of the Regiment. After Sedgemoor Sergeant Weems received a bounty of £40 for firing the 'great guns', not the last time elements of the Regiment were to act as gunners.

The following year, 1686, the Regiment was once again divided into two battalions and, alone among British regiments, was not to have less until after the Second World War. The 2nd Battalion was sent briefly to Scotland, the first time any part of the Regiment had served there, but by 1688 had rejoined the 1st Battalion in the south of England. When Prince William of Orange landed at Torbay in that year the Regiment was among the troops sent to oppose him. As desertions mounted James retired eastwards, but the Regiment remained loyal and anxious to fight, and was at Windsor when the king eventually fled.

William, however, thought highly of the Royal Regiment, and as the Earl of Dumbarton had accompanied the fleeing monarch he appointed his most famous Dutch general, the Duke of Schomberg, to the Colonelcy. This was too much for the Regiment, which decided by a majority to march for Scotland and declared itself ready to die for the Stewarts. The mutiny was shortlived as the Regiment surrendered when surrounded by a greatly superior force of Dutch and English cavalry at Sleaford, but it was nevertheless important as it led directly to the passing of the Mutiny Act. The Regiment escaped lightly with only mild punishments for a few ringleaders. William had no desire to deal harshly and in fact expressed his admiration for 'the firm loyalty and attachment evinced by the Royal Regiment to their former Sovereign when he was forsaken by almost every other person'.

The chief purpose of William's invasion of England had been not so much to sieze the throne as to establish British support for his struggles against France. In accordance with this policy the Regiment was moved to Flanders in 1689 and 1690, the first battalion arriving in time to participate in the Battle of Walcourt. The Regiment was not thereafter involved in any major action until Steenkirk in 1692, by which time Sir Robert Douglas of Glenbervie was Colonel, having succeeded the Duke of Schomberg, who had been killed at the Battle of the Boyne in 1690.

The Battle of Steenkirk was in fact a defeat because of bad generalship but the 1st Battalion distinguished itself by driving four French battalions successively from behind four separate hedges. During one of the French counterattacks the Regiment lost a colour. Seeing this, Sir Robert Douglas jumped over a hedge and recaptured the colour singlehanded, killing the French officer, and, though mortally wounded by a French marksman, threw it back over the hedge to the safety of his own troops.

Sir Robert Douglas was succeeded by Lord George Hamilton,

later first Earl of Orkney, who commanded the Regiment in their next major action, the Battle of Neer Landen, in the following year. This was also a victory for the French, who were considerably superior in numbers, but again the Regiment performed very creditably. Defending a key position at the village of Neer Winden, together with two other battalions, they held off four French brigades before having to retire together with the rest of the army after nightfall.

The Siege of Namur in 1695 marked the last important engagement of the war for the Regiment, and for its services, which included beating off a relieving force, it was awarded the battle honour 'Namur'. The action at Namur was very typical of the sieges of the day in that, despite the bloodiness of the fighting, the garrison were allowed to surrender and march out with honours of war, i.e. bearing arms, colours flying, drums beating, matches lighted and bullet in the mouth. This was in accordance with the understood rules governing the conduct of sieges. If garrisons surrendered they were almost always granted the right to march out with honours of war. If they did not surrender, the town or fortress, when taken, was usually given over to pillage. It was thus no dishonour to surrender, provided resistance was maintained until the last moment before the launching of the final, inevitably successful, assault. The secret of successful defence lay in the correct recognition of this moment since the penalties for misjudgement were high.

After Namur Orkney's Regiment had a short rest from active service during which the first recorded regimental court martial took place in 1700. Two men were charged with desertion and one with forgery and, all pleading guilty, the deserters were sentenced to run the 'Gauntlope' three times and the forger four times after which they were to be dishonourably discharged. The punishment was administered by the entire Regiment, using willow wands or similar switches. The offender was marched down the ranks stripped to the waist while drums were beaten to drown his cries.

The following year, 1701, on the outbreak of the War of the

Spanish Succession, the Regiment resumed active service, sailing to the Netherlands from Ireland, where it had spent the previous three years. By this time all troops, including grenadiers, had been issued with bayonets, and tactics were considerably influenced thereby. Bayonets are first mentioned in 1689, but their value only became apparent with the abolition of pikes during the wars of 1701–13, the old combination of pike and musket being replaced by the single weapon. This simplified the drill and training and enabled the five- or six-rank formation to be reduced to one of three ranks, doubling the firepower of a battalion and increasing its powers of resistance. Without the need for co-ordinating the different weapons of a battalion, there was more concentration on co-operation between cavalry and infantry.

The War of the Spanish Succession opened for the Regiment with the usual round of sieges in the Netherlands. However, in 1704 Marlborough finally broke free from the hampering influence of the Dutch and marched south with an army which included the Royal Regiment. The campaign opened with the Battle of Schellenberg and culminated at Blenheim, in both of which the Regiment was very much to the fore. Marlborough then returned to Holland, where his troops continued to triumph under his inspired leadership. The Regiment fought at Helixem in 1705, at Ramillies in 1706 and then, after a brief return to England occasioned by threats of a Stewart invasion, was engaged at the victories of Oudenarde and Malplaquet in 1708 and '09. In between these major engagements the Regiment was involved in several important sieges.

The record of the Royal Regiment during this particularly famous period in British military history was thus a proud one, and it was deservedly rewarded with the battle honours of 'Blenheim', 'Ramillies', 'Oudenarde' and 'Malplaquet'. Not surprisingly such honours were not won without loss. The casualties at Schellenberg amounted to between a third and a half of the regimental strength. At Blenheim they were equally severe. As a result of these losses Englishmen were recruited to the Regiment for the first time. In the later battles the Regiment suffered less, and at Malplaquet, the scene of the severest fighting of the war, they escaped remarkably lightly as they fought the whole day in a wood.

Malplaquet must nevertheless have been a memorable battle for a certain Private McBain of the Regiment. He made money in winter by running fencing schools in the towns where he was quartered, and managed to support a wife and child in Flanders. But when his wife decided to go home she had the infant delivered to its father. It reached him on parade just before the Battle of Malplaquet and, having no other place to put it, McBain fought the entire battle with the child in his knapsack.

Private McBain's winter activities were not all that unusual. While in winter quarters the troops lived much as civilians; parades were few and men were often attended by their wives, as well as numerous other civilian followers and servants. Such was the attendant retinue that restrictions even had to be placed on the number of horses per regiment. Many officers spent much of the winter on leave, and parties of officers and NCOs toured the country at home on recruiting trips. Those wanting 'sport', and a chance of profit, could obtain a licence from their garrison commander to raid the enemy. If a senior officer was captured his ransom was divided among the raiding party. The severity of the fighting was thus to some extent offset by the lighthearted approach to campaigning in general.

While the War of the Spanish Succession raged abroad, at home the Union of Scotland and England was completed in 1707, and accordingly the Cross of St George and the Cross of St Andrew were combined on regimental colours. The Royal Regiment's badge was also altered from the thistle and crown surrounded by the inscription 'Nemo me impune lacessit' to the Royal Cypher within the circle of St Andrew, surmounted by a crown.

The period following the War of the Spanish Succession was one of little activity for the Regiment. The Treaty of Utrecht was signed in 1713, and by 1715 the Regiment was on garrison duty in Ireland, where it was to remain until 1742. One of the reasons for its original posting to Ireland was to prevent any rising by the Roman Catholics there in sympathy with the Old Pretender. However, his cause was in fact espoused by at least one member of the Regiment, Ensign Lord George Murray, who was to act as a Lieutenant-General for the Young Pretender in the '45 Rebellion.

At this time dress was very much as it had been on the introduction of the red coat. The coat was worn unbuttoned at the neck and chest over a waistcoat made out of the previous year's coat. Hats, instead of being loose-brimmed, were laced up to form the three-cornered hat. Clothes were issued yearly, as follows: 'A good full bod'd cloth coat, well lined, which may serve for the waistcoat the second year; a waistcoat; a pair of good kersey breeches; a pair of good strong stockings; a pair of good strong shoes; two good shirts and two neckloths; a good strong hat, well laced.'

The uniform was not good enough for at least one man in the Regiment, Sergeant Donald Macleod, who in 1730 obtained his discharge to join the kilted Black Watch. He fought with the Royals throughout Marlborough's campaigns and, being an extremely good swordsman, kept his hand in with duels in between the battles. He campaigned against the rebels in 1715 and distinguished himself at Sheriffmuir where he was wounded. After joining the Black Watch he was wounded again, at Fontenoy, but nothing daunted then transferred to Fraser's Highlanders and was engaged at Louisburg and at Quebec where he was wounded in two places. Returning to Britain as part of the guard over General Wolfe's body he was admitted as a Chelsea Pensioner in 1759, at the age of 71. On recovering from his wounds, however, he volunteered once more, joining Campbell's Highlanders with whom he was twice wounded in Germany. He finally retired to the Highlands in 1776 when he was 88 and, although he was shipwrecked and lost all his money, lived to the age of 103.

Despite his wounds Sergeant Macleod could consider himself

lucky to escape the fate of the 2nd Battalion, which in 1741 was sent to Jamaica, arriving there in 1742. This posting marked a new departure for the Regiment. Hitherto both battalions had generally served together or in close proximity. They had fought in the same countries and in the same campaigns, if often in different brigades. From 1742 they were usually separated and posted far apart. It was now, too, that the first references to The Royal Scots, or The Scots Royals, appear, but their official name remained The Royal Regiment.

The expedition to Spanish America was a complete débâcle. The Regiment arrived in time to add its complement of fit men to a force sent to capture Porto Bello, but after nineteen days at sea in bad weather the casualties from disease, aggravated by the cramped conditions of shipboard life, were so high that the expedition was abandoned. Yellow fever, not the Spaniards, was the real enemy. By the end of the year it had won; all troops were withdrawn, but of the original force only one man in ten survived to reach England alive.

Shortly after the return of the 2nd Battalion, which was now placed on the British, as opposed to the Irish, establishment, the 1st Battalion was sent to Germany to serve in the War of the Austrian Succession. It arrived just too late to take part in the Battle of Dettingen in 1743, but was heavily involved in the Battle of Fontenoy in 1745. Casualties were very high, over a third of the Battalion, in this action during which General Moltke described The Royals as 'behaving like lions'.

Later in the same year the Battalion found itself made prisoner-of-war as a result of marching to the relief of Ghent, in the face of considerable opposition, and arriving there in insufficient force only the day before the town surrendered. The Battalion was duly exchanged, and returned to England for a short period, during which it was involved in various raids against the French coast. The war culminated for the Battalion in 1747 with the relief of Hulst and the defence of Fort Sandberg. Fighting at both these actions was very severe. At Fort Sandberg, owing to the flight of a Dutch battalion, the main French assault fell on The Royals, and in the night street fighting which followed the Battalion lost over half its strength.

While the 1st Battalion was fighting abroad the Young Pretender had raised his standard at home, thus initiating what was in some respects another aspect of the continental struggle. There were few troops in Britain at the time, but in August of 1745 two raw companies of The Royals, while on their way to reinforce the garrison at Fort William, came into unexpectedly early contact with the rebels, were ambushed by them and forced to surrender. The subsequent progress of the rebellion led to the 2nd Battalion's recall from Ireland to join the army assembling under General Wade in Yorkshire. The Battalion reached Scotland with the rest of the army in early 1746. In mid-January they were part of a force engaged at Falkirk and, though beaten, retired on Edinburgh in good order.

The highlanders also retired after Falkirk, northwards to Inverness. The royal army followed them, not through the Highlands but via Aberdeen. There was some stiff marching in heavy weather on rations of little more than bread and water, but the rebels were finally engaged at Culloden Moor in April. There survives an account of the battle by a Private Taylor of the Regiment:

'It was a very cold morning and nothing to buy or comfort us; but we had the ammunition loaf, thank God; but not a dram of brandy or spirits had you given a crown for a gill, not nothing but the loaf and water. We had also the greatest difficulty in keeping the locks of our firelocks dry, for the rain was violent. The battle began by cannonading and continued for half an hour or more with great guns. But our gunners galling their lines, they betook themselves to their small arms, sword and pistol, and came running to our front like troops of hungry wolves, and fought with intrepidity.'

However, the highlanders were in an even worse state, having nothing to eat, and above all no cannon with which to reply to the royal force's bombardment. Not surprisingly the battle only lasted an hour and the 2nd Battalion's casualties were just four men missing.

After the Battle of Culloden the 2nd Battalion remained in Scotland for a couple of years before joining the 1st Battalion in Ireland in 1749. In 1751, while The Royals were on garrison duty there, the army was numbered and thereafter the Regiment was officially designated the First or Royal Regiment of Foot. There followed a period of relative peace for the Regiment which was broken in 1757 when the 2nd Battalion was posted to Halifax in Nova Scotia. The Regiment's last battles had been its only fighting ever on its native Scottish soil, and must thereby have provided all the greater contrast to its posting to the New World, for, while the Regiment had been across the Atlantic before, it was now going in earnest and for no brief period.

The Peace of Aix-la-Chapelle in 1748 had ended the War of the Austrian Succession, but it had not settled the chief issue between France and England, that of colonial supremacy. The fighting in India and America, if not officially recognized, had never ceased, and with the outbreak of the Seven Years War in 1756 it was given fresh impetus. The British effort was almost entirely concentrated on operations overseas and it was in further-ance of this policy that most of the Regiment's active service in the next 35 years was to be in the New World.

Chapter 3

THE 2nd Battalion arrived in Halifax in the middle of 1757, but was not immediately involved in any action. The rest of the year and the winter were spent in preparation for an attack on Louisburg, and apparently well spent, for when a force moved against the fortress the following summer it surrendered in little over a month. Over 5,000 prisoners were captured, as well as large quantities of stores and arms, and 'Louisburg' was awarded as a battle honour. The Battalion's losses, though, were remarkably slight, only fifteen killed and thirty-one wounded.

The success at Louisburg was followed up in 1759, when a force moved up Lake Champlain, using blankets as sails, and forced the French to abandon the forts of Ticonderoga and Crown Point. The ease with which these forts were taken was in sharp contrast to the previous year when the Black Watch had suffered appalling losses after being quite unnecessarily ordered to make a frontal assault on Fort Ticonderoga.

The Battalion wintered in New Jersey. Thereafter the history of its campaigning in America is diverse, as it was split up for service in widely differing parts of the continent. In 1760 six companies, including two light companies, embarked from New York for Charleston in South Carolina. There they formed part of a force operating against the Cherokees. The weather was hot and long marches had to be made over difficult terrain. Moreover the Indians, skilled at making use of the country, exacted rather more casualties than had the French, so that tactics had to be altered, with the emphasis on an open formation and the use of light companies for scouting.

After the first expedition, which achieved little, the two light companies returned to New York to join the rest of the Battalion. The four remaining companies wintered in Charleston and then marched against the Indians again in 1761. The operations lasted longer and conditions were even more severe than the previous year, but on this occasion the primary object was achieved in that the Cherokees agreed to peace terms. The detachment remained in South Carolina one more year before sailing for Barbados in 1762.

Meanwhile the rest of the Battalion formed part of the force that took Montreal in September of 1760. With the fall of Montreal Britain won the struggle for Canada as thereafter French resistance ceased. The two light companies temporarily posted to South Carolina had by that time rejoined the Canadian force. In 1761, however, when four companies sailed from New York for Guadaloupe the two light companies, together with the grenadier company, were once again detached, and stayed at Montreal.

Guadaloupe had been captured in 1759 and was used as a base from which the island of Dominica was attacked in 1761, The four companies formed part of the attacking force, which completed its task successfully, with little loss, and then moved to Barbados. From Barbados Martinique was attacked and taken in 1762 by a force including the small contingent of Royals, which was shortly afterwards enlarged by the arrival of the four companies from South Carolina. There was thus nearly a full battalion to participate in the major operation of 1762, the attack on Havana. Havana was well fortified, the key point in the defences being Fort Moro. The fort was besieged for six weeks under very adverse conditions due to hard ground, heat and lack of water, in addition to the counter-attacks of the Spaniards, but was eventually taken by an assault in which The Royals played a leading part, suffering most of the casualties. After the fall of Fort Moro the town was taken with little trouble, and the Regiment was granted 'Havannah' as a battle honour.

The three companies left in Montreal had not been idle while the rest of the Battalion was in the West Indies. They formed part of the force that recaptured St John's, Newfoundland, in late 1762, afer it had been captured by an expeditionary force sent

B

from France. The detached companies were re-united with the rest of the Battalion at Carlisle the following year, when home service was resumed at the end of the Seven Years War.

While the 2nd Battalion had been in North America and the West Indies the 1st Battalion had remained on garrison duty in Ireland. The only notable occurrence in this uneventful period was in 1760 when the Battalion embarked at Cork in five small boats for a raid on the French coast. However, the force did nothing except lie off Quiberon Bay for three weeks before being ordered to return home.

After the end of the war the 1st Battalion stayed on in Ireland while the 2nd was posted to Scotland. Both Battalions remained in their respective areas until 1768, the 2nd being split up into detachments which served in various parts of Scotland. At this time Scotland was still in the grip of the repression that followed the '45, when even the wearing of Highland garb was forbidden, so the Battalion was to some extent regarded as an occupying force. Nevertheless the country was gradually being re-organized under a single system of government, with the highlanders as tenants of their clan chiefs. While one result was the infamy of the 'clearances' the system did produce the famous Highland Regiments and achieved some degree of unity and co-operation. This was in sharp contrast to Ireland where the lack of co-operation across the barriers of class, property and religion was to lead to such trouble in the future.

The Battalion strength at this time was, as usual, reduced after the cessation of hostilities. Each battalion had 9 companies of between 40 and 50 men including a light and grenadier company. The two specialist companies were undoubtedly useful in their respective spheres, scouting and assault work, but they showed how once again tactical developments were influencing the internal organization of the Battalion, in this case complicating the straightforward system that had been introduced with the bayonet.

The developments in the organization of the Battalion were mirrored in the uniform which became steadily more ornate from about 1740 onwards. The red coats were worn open in front, and were turned back at the chest to show royal blue facings. The skirts were also buttoned back in order to free the knees. The waistcoat, being exposed, became more decorated. The stockings were replaced by white gaiters, reaching to above the knee, which were worn with red breeches (blue for grenadiers). Around 1760 the waistcoat and breeches became white and the gaiters black, the coat being also lined with white. Further changes took place towards the end of the century when the coat that buttoned back at the knees was replaced by a form of tail coat, and gaiters were shortened to just below the knee. 1768 saw the three-cornered hat replaced by a two-cornered one, but with exaggerated projections at the sides. The grenadier's high pointed cloth hat also changed, becoming a high furred hat. Hair, which had been short, was worn long, with a powdered queue.

The increasing decoration and complexity of the uniform was merely a reflection of what was happening to civilian dress. However, while civilian wages increased proportionately a private soldier's wage was still only £12 3s 4d a year. After official, and unofficial, deductions he only received about 2s 6d a week with which, in the words of an official document of the time, 'to fill his belly, wash his linnen, shave his beard, powder his hair, black his shoes, colour his accoutrements, etc etc.' Nor was the situation substantially improved until near the end of the century.

Changes in uniform took some time to affect troops serving abroad so that on its return to England the 2nd Battalion may well have found itself dressed somewhat differently from the 1st. In 1768, however, it was the turn of the latter to be posted overseas, to Gibraltar, while the 2nd Battalion moved south to England. After three years in England it too moved to the Mediterranean, to Minorca. Both then stayed at their overseas posts until recalled to England in 1775 on the outbreak of war with the American Colonies.

The year 1776 saw both Battalions on guard and garrison

duty near London, in close proximity to each other for the first time for nearly 20 years. During the next four years both remained on home service, doing duty throughout the country, but most frequently near London. In 1780 the 1st Battalion finally sailed for the West Indies. The 2nd formed part of the troops stationed in and around London during the riots of that year. It found guards at the royal palaces, and was frequently inspected, always receiving high praise. It is significant that the entire Regiment remained on home service for all but two years of the American Revolutionary Wars of 1775–82. It was a difficult period for Britain as much because of internal discontent and riots against Parliament as because of foreign problems. Thus the troops maintaining order at home were performing as vital a service as those fighting abroad.

However, by the time the 1st Battalion did sail for the West Indies Britain was effectively at war with Holland, Sweden, Denmark, Russia and Prussia, as well as with the American Colonies, France and Spain. It was thus against the Dutch possessions in the West Indies that the British effort was directed. The Battalion formed part of a force that took the islands of St Eustasia, St Mark and Saba in early 1781, in conjunction with the Navy under Admiral Rodney. The Battalion, together with some artillery and engineers, was then left as a holding force on the nearby island of St Christopher.

In early 1782 a French fleet arrived at the island with a greatly superior force of about 8,000 troops. Unable to oppose a landing the Battalion withdrew to the entrenched position of Brimstone Hill at one end of the island. The French rapidly besieged the position, and though Admiral Hood managed to land a relieving force it was too weak to be of use. The strength of the defenders was reduced to 500 before they eventually surrendered, having held the position for just on a month. The garrison was allowed to march out with honours of war, on the usual condition that it was out of action till exchanged.

The Battalion, after being exchanged, returned to England the same year, and was almost immediately engaged in the suppression of riots around Coventry. The following year, 1793, it was posted to Ireland, and the year after the 2nd Battalion was also posted there. Considering how frequent was the Regiment's service in Ireland during this period the number of Irishmen in the ranks was surprisingly low. In 1787 the figures for distribution of nationalities were: 1st Battalion – Scots 262, English 51, Irish 60; 2nd Battalion – Scots 231, English 99, Irish 53.

An outstanding regimental character at this time was 'Big Sam McDonald'. He stood 6' 10" and was as strong as he was tall. One of the many stories told of him relates how he was posted sentry on a field gun. When the orderly officer went on his rounds he was surprised to find neither sentry nor gun. On going into the guardroom he found that Sam, feeling cold, had carried the gun into the guardroom and was sitting over it beside the fire.

However much characters like Sam McDonald helped to liven up the more boring periods of service, that from 1782 to 1793, between the American Revolutionary Wars and the French Revolutionary Wars, must have been particularly galling for the Regiment. Army strength was allowed to lapse even more than was usual in time of peace and the figures given for the distribution for nationalities show the extent by which the Regiment's personnel was reduced. Even on the outbreak of war with France, when strengths had been increased in anticipation of hostilities, the 1st Battalion still had only 400 men and the 2nd 420.

When war was declared in 1793 the 1st Battalion was in Jamaica, having been sent there on garrison duty in 1790. The West Indies were becoming increasingly important, both for their own products and because they lay on or near so many of the trade routes to the American mainland. All the Sea Powers had colonies among them, St Domingo being the chief French island. In early 1793 French Republican agents instigated a revolt among the slaves of the island. The French on the island appealed to the Governor of Jamaica for help and he responded by sending a force, though of necessity it was somewhat limited as he had only 19 weak battalions at his disposal.

The 1st Battalion was sent to St Domingo as a reinforcement the following year. Throughout its service in the island it was split into detachments, sometimes numbering as many as seven. Most of the detachments helped at the capture of Fort L'Acal and then at the siege and capture of Port au Prince. One detachment distinguished itself as part of a force, 120 strong, which held Fort Bizzeton against attacks by over 2,000.

Despite such successes the British forces were withdrawn from the island in 1796, once again defeated not by the enemy but by disease, striking this time with catastrophic effect. In the three years up to 1796 the British lost 40,000 men in the West Indies, without noticeably affecting the course of the war. Of the force sent to St Domingo nearly 6,000 officers and men died from disease; battle losses were only about 100. The Royals, whose strength sank to below 100 on occasion, lost five officers and 400 men, and the Battalion eventually returned to England in 1797 with a total strength of 170 men. It was not surprising that it was immediately posted to Scotland to recruit.

After the 1st Battalion had been posted to Jamaica the 2nd remained in Ireland until it was sent to Gibraltar in 1793, just before the outbreak of war. Later in the same year the Battalion moved to Toulon, which had rebelled against the Republicans, as part of the small British contingent among the heterogenous forces defending the city. The Battalion was assigned to the 15-mile-long Fort Mulgrave sector, defending it successfully, as well as taking part in an effective but costly raid on the French guns, which had been causing great damage under the direction of a certain Napoleon Buonaparte.

By the end of the year, however, Toulon was abandoned, and in early 1794 the Battalion was sent to Corsica, where, as part of a force under the command of Lieutenant-Colonel (later Sir John) Moore, it helped to capture Fort Martello and Farinole, so that Martello Bay could be used as a fleet base. After taking part in the campaigns in the rest of the island the Battalion was then garrisoned in the towns of Bastia and Calvi until Corsica also was abandoned in 1796.

The British force in Corsica moved to Elba, from which in 1797 the Battalion was sent to Lisbon. From Lisbon it returned very briefly to England in 1799 before setting out for Holland as part of a Scottish brigade under Major-General John Moore. The British forces landed at Kieck Down against weak opposition, and the following day the Battalion, together with the 2nd Battalion Gordon Highlanders, took Helder Fort, which commanded the Dutch fleet, whose surrender followed shortly afterwards. The campaign culminated at the Battle of Egmont-op-Zee, in which the Battalion made an extremely successful bayonet attack, for which they were awarded a battle honour, but the British forces were then withdrawn as the anticipated Dutch rising against the French had not materialized.

The first half of the year 1800 saw both battalions in England, the 1st having returned from Ireland, to which it had been sent during the rebellion of 1798 and 1799. The 2nd stayed in England till August, when it sailed for Spain, having lost three officers, four NCOs and thirty-two men to a new experimental battalion of riflemen that was eventually to become the Rifle Brigade. The Spanish expedition proved abortive; the Battalion landed twice, only to be withdrawn almost immediately on each occasion. Eventually the entire expeditionary force moved on to Malta via Gibraltar.

By this time the tunic with tails had become the established uniform. It was buttoned from neck to waist, thus eliminating facings, and was worn with tight white breeches which buttoned outside the knees. Hair was still long, with a ten inch queue, but powder had been abolished in 1797. In 1800 the cocked hat gave way to a cylindrical high black shako with plume and peak. Thus arrayed the Regiment faced the new century and with it the Napoleonic Wars, which were to provide the background to some of the most famous victories in its history.

Chapter 4

URING the Napoleonic Wars the Regiment was raised for
the first time to a strength of four battalions. However,
the third and fourth Battalions were not recruited until
1804 and did not see action until some time after that. Thus for
the early part of the war The Royals were still only represented by
the two battalions in existence in 1800.

The 1st Battalion spent the entire period of the war in the
Americas. It was sent to the West Indies in early 1801, and on
arrival participated in the capture of St Martin, St Thomas, St
John and Santa Cruz. The Battalion was then split into detachments in order to garrison these islands, which it continued to
do until 1803, with a short break in 1802 when the islands were
briefly returned to France after the Peace of Amiens. 1803 saw
the Battalion stationed in St Kitts and Antigua before concentra-
ting at Barbados for an attack on the Dutch settlements in
Guiana. On taking these, the Battalion, less two companies left
in Antigua, remained in the area on garrison duty until 1812.
Some of the detachments, in particular those on the island of
Tobago, overlapped with those of the 2nd Battalion, which was
also in the West Indies for part of the war.

The grenadier and light companies were the only units of the
1st Battalion which were actively engaged during this period; they
helped take Guadeloupe from the French (for the third time) in
1810. Otherwise the Battalion's only enemies were boredom, and,
as usual, disease. T. S. St Clair, who joined the Battalion as a
lieutenant in 1806 and was stationed in Demerara and Berbice,
notes in his memoirs that, 'The yellow fever, which has so
fatally raged in the islands, has very rarely made its appearance
in this part of the South American continent.' Later he says,
'The prevailing diseases in this country are flux, disentery, cholic,
fevers, and liver complaints. They seldom prove fatal if attended

to in the commencement.' Lieutenant St Clair's remarks are, however, at variance with what would now be regarded as a high mortality rate, 166 men dying of disease in eight months in 1805. Despite these trying conditions the Battalion bore up well and maintained a high standard of discipline and morale.

In 1812 the Battalion assembled at Barbados, prior to leaving the West Indies. There it was inspected by the GOC who pronounced it unfit for active service as a result of its eleven-year stay in the Caribbean. Nevertheless it sailed for Quebec for service in the war against America. Detachments were present at many of the numerous engagements around Lake Ontario in 1813. Some troops even acted as marines on British ships on the lake, and the grenadier company participated in the successful surprise attack on Fort Niagara in December of that year.

Having come straight from the West Indies the Battalion inevitably suffered greatly from the severity of the winter climate. But in 1814 it was once more very actively engaged, mostly in the operations centred on Fort Erie. The Battalion covered the retreat from the fort, eventually checking the American advance at Lundy's Lane, 'A service which this valuable corps executed with great steadiness'. For its part in the war, which ended in December, the Battalion won for the Regiment the honour 'Niagara'. Although the campaigns in which the 1st Battalion was engaged went unsung and unnoticed, as compared with the campaigns in which other parts of the Regiment were involved, it had seen some of the most unpleasant service of the war, and it must have been a great relief to the survivors when they eventually sailed for home in January, 1815.

By the time the 1st Battalion had set off for the West Indies the 2nd Battalion, together with the rest of the force originally sent against Spain, was fully engaged in preparations for the invasion of Egypt. To this end the force sailed from Malta for Marmorice Bay in Asia Minor, which they reached in December, 1800. After some weeks spent practising landing in the face of an enemy the invasion force embarked and arrived before Alexandria in March. There the training in Marmorice Bay paid off, for, despite fierce resistance, a beachhead was established, the 2nd Battalion distinguishing itself on the left flank. During the advance on Alexandria the Battalion was engaged in several sharp skirmishes; it was part of the force that took Cairo in June and it was present at the fall of Alexandria in September when the French evacuated Egypt.

As a result of the Egyptian actions the Regiment was awarded the honour of the Sphinx with the superscription 'Egypt'. The Battalion's next posting provided an unfortunate contrast, for it spent the whole of 1802 in Gibraltar. At that time the station was notoriously bad for discipline. 'Immorality, laxity of all military rule and insubordination among the men prevailed to an alarming extent. The troops on parade presented a slovenly appearance and want of uniformity in their dress and appointments, while inaccuracy in their movements was apparent to any observer. Discipline was at the lowest ebb, the men were often in a disgraceful state of intoxication and no unprotected female could walk the streets, even in the daytime, without being subject to insult, and sometimes brutal violence.' Shortly after the Battalion's arrival Edward, Duke of Kent, the father of Queen Victoria, who had become Colonel of the Regiment in 1801, was sent out as Governor with orders to restore discipline. His measures aroused such discontent that by Christmas men of The Royals broke into open mutiny, which climaxed with the grenadier company being compelled to open fire on them. After discipline had been enforced by a series of court martials, the following year the Battalion was sent to England, and then on to the West Indies.

As soon as it arrived in Barbados the Battalion was ordered to the attack on St Lucia, and won the battle honour 'St Lucia' for its part in the capture of the island. After then helping to take Tobago, the Battalion was posted on garrison duty in various islands and in some of the outposts in Dutch Guiana, when, as mentioned, it came into contact with detachments of the 1st Battalion. After two years of such duty it left for home in 1805. Before sailing, all the fit men were transferred to the 1st Battalion, so that the 2nd Battalion arrived in England in 1806 with a total strength of 72, of which only six officers, eleven sergeants, a drummer and a private were fit.

The Battalion, after a year in England recruiting, spent most of 1807 en route for India, the first time in its 175-year history that any part of the Regiment had been there. The voyage out, in the usual small transports, was particularly uncomfortable for one party whose rations were so short that there was an outbreak of scurvy. Another ship carrying the grenadier company leaked so much that it had to put in at Rio de Janeiro for repairs. It did not reach Madras until February, 1808, having lost one man to hostile natives on an island where the ship put in for fresh water.

The 2nd Battalion stayed in India until 1831, but was not involved in any major campaign until 1817. Life was nevertheless extremely harsh. Only very limited forces were available to cover all of the Madras Presidency, Mysore and Hyderabad, and the Battalion spent most of the time marching, either from one post to another, or against bandits and raiders. The marches usually started at three in the morning and lasted for between six and eight hours. The roads were so narrow that troops often had to move in single file, and in the rice-growing areas they were so wet that many marched barefoot.

If the marches were bad, living quarters were equally so. According to a sergeant of the Regiment barracks were 'very temporary, being entirely made from the cocoanut tree, and were divided into five houses clear from end to end and each containing 180 men.' 'Beds were as temporary as the barracks, being stakes driven into the ground and spaked* over from end to end like a horse's rack for holding hay, without any bedding whatever.' As for rations, 'we were served out with buffalo beef on which there was not to be seen a shred of fat and rice was our substitute for bread.' The conditions, combined with the climate and the high incidence of disease, wreaked a daily toll. On one occasion, shortly after its arrival in India, the Battalion was

* Spake: bamboo lathe.

ordered to march to the coast for health reasons. The idea was abandoned after heat stroke brought down 300, killing 12, on the first march.

One of the few consolations under such conditions was that at least uniforms had become more sensible as a result of the years of war. In India the clothing was of thin material. The red coat was light and loose with short tails, and was worn open necked. The shako remained, but with a cotton flap to protect the back of the head and neck. Pigtails had gone, and breeches and leggings were replaced by trousers, grey in Europe and white cotton in India.

Europe, which saw nothing of the 1st and 2nd Battalions during the Napoleonic Wars, was almost the only theatre of war for the 3rd and 4th Battalions. Of these the 4th Battalion had much the quieter time. After its formation in 1804 it remained at home supplying drafts for the rest of the Regiment for 9 years. In 1812 the Regiment's title was changed to The 1st Regiment of Foot, The Royal Scots, and it was thus for the first time officially designated 'Royal Scots'. In the same year the 4th Battalion was sent to join the expedition to Swedish Pomerania.

The Battalion arrived at Lubeck and spent some weeks there before its plans were changed and it was ordered to Holland to help the Dutch in their uprising against the French. The Battalion therefore set off from Lubeck in January, reaching Holland in early March, despite extremely severe conditions (on one occasion 120 men were lost in a snowstorm). After this unpleasant march the Battalion was only involved in one action, the surprise attack on the fortress of Bergen-op-Zoom, when it crossed the River Zoom and forced an entry through the water gate. Unfortunately the rest of the attack failed, so that, after maintaining its position against strong opposition all night, the Battalion, faced by greatly superior forces, including artillery, and with its retreat cut off by the rise of the tide in the Zoom, was forced to surrender.

After being duly exchanged the 4th Battalion sailed for Quebec, their troubles by no means at an end. One transport,

HMS *Diomede*, reached Quebec safely. The other, HMS *Leopard*, after running aground on the Isle of Wight, underwent a very stormy crossing, only to strike hard on a reef in a fog in the St Lawrence. All on board were transferred to Anticosti Island nearby, but there they had to remain for a fortnight before being rescued, by which time all rations except rum were very short. Even then the Battalion remained unlucky as one of the rescue ships was involved in a collision with HMS *Diomede* and only just reached Quebec.

The Battalion was assembled in Quebec by July, but again the unpleasant journey was to be followed by little in the way of action, for the American war ended in December. The following year the 1st and 4th Battalions returned to England together, and the 4th Battalion was posted to Paris to join the 3rd Battalion as part of the army of occupation. After a year in France the Battalion returned to England and was disbanded in 1816.

The 4th Battalion had achieved little despite the expenditure of considerable effort but for this it could not be blamed. Sir Denis Pack, its Brigade Commander in France, expressed himself confident that 'they would have emulated their comrades in the 3rd Battalion, had the same glorious opportunity been afforded them'.

The history of the 3rd Battalion provided a sharp contrast to that of the 4th. Also founded in 1804 the 3rd Battalion first saw action in 1808. Towards the end of that year it renewed the Regiment's association with Sir John Moore when, as part of the expeditionary force under his overall command, it sailed for Corunna in Spain. After landing, the British troops marched inland, unaware that the Spanish army had already been defeated by a very strong French army commanded by Napoleon in person. It was thanks to a Captain Waters of The Royals that the true situation was discovered. In the words of Colonel Simson:

'He was riding ahead with the cavalry and arrived in a village to find that a French officer had just been killed and the

Spaniards were searching his saddle bags, in which were despatches. After a long haggle Captain Waters bought them for twenty dollars. The French officer had ridden up to the inn demanding fresh horses, but the innkeeper was busy dancing with a Spanish girl among a crowd outside, the day being a festival. The innkeeper refused to do anything till his dance was finished, whereupon the French officer seized hold of him and was promptly stabbed by the Spanish lady.'

In the face of the French forces the British had to retire 250 miles on Corunna. Conditions on the retreat were extremely harsh and exhausting because of the mountainous terrain and the bad, snow-covered roads, but on reaching Corunna a counter-attack had to be launched to cover the embarkation of the British troops. For their part in this famous action, which cost Sir John Moore his life, The Royals were awarded the battle honour 'Corunna'.

However, the 3rd Battalion had not won its first laurels lightly; during the short-lived Spanish expedition it had lost over 40 per cent of its strength. It was not an easy time for recruiting and though men were supplied from the other battalions of the Regiment, by the time the 3rd Battalion was back to full strength it could only number 55 Scots, with 400 Irish and 650 English. The high casualty rate, the expansion of the army and the increase in the number of battalions during the Napoleonic Wars called for more men than Scotland could provide. As a result, for the first time the number of Scotsmen in the Regiment ceased to predominate. The number in the 3rd Battalion after Corunna, though, was quite exceptionally low. Very much more typical was the distribution in the 2nd Battalion in 1814: 315 Scots, 352 English and 515 Irish. The large number of Irish was an indirect result of the Irish rebellion of 1798–9 after which many Irish volunteered for the British Army.

The 3rd Battalion had only a short respite before going into action again. In July it joined the expedition against the Dutch island of Walcheren, in the mouth of the River Scheldt. The bulk of the Battalion embarked on the HMS *Revenge*, and while still at Portsmouth there occurred an incident which is quoted by Private Douglas, who has left memoirs of his service with the Battalion, as an example of the extremely strict discipline enforced by Lieutenant-Colonel Hay. Apparently there was some discussion as to whether a soldier could be punished with the cat-o'-nine-tails. In due course a Corporal Frazer was so punished, for arguing with a midshipman, and consequently he appealed to Lieutenant-Colonel Hay. Hay, far from sympathizing with the victim, ordered a parade and, addressing the corporal, said, 'You have written to me complaining of being punished with sailor's cats, and by God, if you do not behave better in future I will hang you with sailor's ropes.'

Apart from this incident the voyage passed uneventfully and after an unopposed landing the British force advanced on Flushing. Sickness, caused by the damp climate, ultimately caused the expedition to be abandoned before the end of the year. However, nothing further had been achieved after the capture of Flushing and the whole affair appears to have been thoroughly mismanaged even before 'Walcheren Fever' took over. Captain St Clair, who had by now joined the 3rd Battalion, contented himself with the temperate comment, 'Pity that with such an armament so little should have been accomplished'. Private Douglas probably better expressed the general feeling amongst those serving on the expedition with his remark, 'Thus terminated in the conquest of a graveyard, one of the finest, as well as one of the worst conducted armaments, that ever England sent from her shores.' He also made some pungent criticisms of the Earl of Chatham's command and pointed out what losses would have been saved in the Peninsula if the Walcheren Expedition, or even a part of it, had been sent South after it was obvious that nothing more was to be achieved in Holland.

Private Douglas's comments were all the more heartfelt in view of the fact that the Peninsula was the Battalion's next scene of action. Despite its sick list it was given less than two months rest before embarking again for Lisbon, which it reached in

April, 1810, with only some 500 fit for strenuous work out of a total strength of just over 800. Fortunately the Battalion did not move into action until September. By that time Massena was approaching the British bases in Portugal and Wellington moved to oppose him at Busaco Ridge. The 5th Division, which included the 3rd Battalion, was on the extreme right and launched the flank attack that won the battle, and also won for the Regiment its first battle honour under Wellington.

The winter was spent quietly behind the lines of Torres Vedras and the following year, 1811, the retreating Massena was followed and beaten at Fuentes d'Onoro. The 3rd Battalion was only very lightly engaged in this battle and saw no other heavy fighting the entire year. However, it was not a pleasant year. Wellington was trying to keep the French guessing and consequently the Battalion spent most of the time engaged in long marches. The terrain was difficult, the tracks bad, the climate extreme and billets poor or non-existent. Rations were a particular source of grievance as they were in very short supply and usually arrived late if at all. Some idea of their quality is given by the following extract from Douglas's memoirs: 'The biscuit when it did arrive was in such a state, owing to the long carriage, and being exposed to all kinds of weather, that no human being (except such as we were) could make use of it. For it actually stank, and when emptied out of the bags, it smoked equal to a dunghill at a stable door. The vegetables round the town soon disappeared, these consisted chiefly of nettles, which were devoured with no bad appetites, and often without salt.' There was one consolation in the middle of the year when a very strong draft of re-inforcements arrived from the 4th Battalion.

The campaigning in 1812 provided a sharp contrast. It opened with the capture of Ciudad Rodrigo, followed by the storming of Badajoz and then the Battle of Salamanca. At the time of Ciudad Rodrigo the Battalion was in reserve with the rest of the 5th Division, and at Badajoz they formed Wellington's personal guard. This spell of relative inactivity was ended at Salamanca where the 5th Division carried out the highly successful counter-

1. 'Big Sam' McDonald beside a six-foot tall Grenadier in 1789.

2. Sir Robert Douglas of Glenbervie recovering the colours at the Battle of Steenkirk, 1692.

3. *A Private beside 'Mons Meg' at Edinburgh Castle in 1846.*

4. *Officers of the 2nd Battalion at Aldershot, 1863.*

5. The 1st Battalion disembarking at Durban for Zululand in 1888.

6. Men of the 3rd Battalion in South Africa during the Boer War.

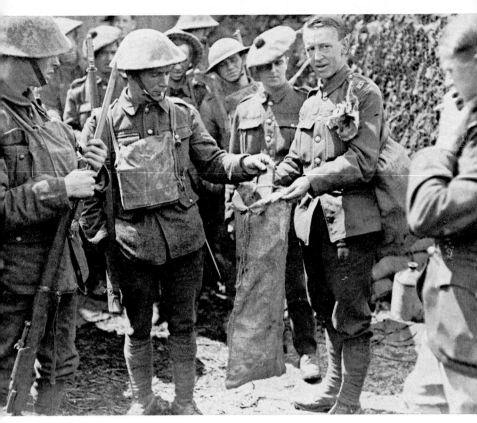

7. *Collecting personal belongings from men of the 11th Battalion about to go out on a daylight raid during the First World War.*

8. *A trench post near Croisilles occupied by the 15th Royal Scots in January, 1918.*

attack which drove the enemy off several ridges in succession, culminating in their complete defeat. The Regiment was awarded the battle honour 'Salamanca' as a result of this engagement and the 3rd Battalion took part in the capture of Burgos which followed. The British then once again retired to Portugal for the winter, the Battalion being detached on the way to cover the destruction of bridges near Palencia and fighting some sharp skirmishes with superior forces of the enemy. By the end of the year's campaigning the 3rd Battalion had 370 fit men and 566 sick.

Fortunately for The Royals the 1813 campaign, which was to provide some of the severest fighting in the 3rd Battalion's history, did not start till May, thus giving the Battalion plenty of time to recoup its strength. The first engagement was the Battle of Vittoria in June. The Battalion participated in a bayonet attack which drove in the enemy right and cut off their retreat. It was then detached with the 5th Division to capture the fortified seaport of San Sebastian and thus open up a short supply route.

The Battle of San Sebastian was an unfortunately protracted affair. After a breach had apparently been opened by bombardment, the 3rd Battalion, together with the 1st Norfolk, led an assault. However, the breach proved not to be a breach at all and the attack was doomed to failure from the start. Nevertheless, although bombarded by their own artillery who had not been given the time of the attack, The Royals pressed on, despite 'a frightful fire of grape, bullets and hand-grenades', and eventually had to be peremptorily ordered to retire. The assault cost the Battalion 333 casualties, including its commanding officer. The GOC 5th Division, Sir Thomas Graham, wrote in his despatch, 'The Royal Regiment proved by the numbers left in the breach that it would have been carried had they not been opposed by real obstacles, which no human powers could overcome.'

After this setback the bombardment continued, but before an assault could be launched on the breach thus opened it was discovered that the French had laid a mine there. In order to precipitate them into firing it seventeen men of The Royals, under Lieutenant Macadam of the 9th Foot, launched what was described as 'one of the most gallant actions on record'. They rushed forward into the breach shouting and cheering and doing their best to imitate a full battalion attack, knowing that if the ruse were to succeed they were almost certain to die. Unfortunately the French were not deceived and all seventeen were shot without causing the mine to be blown. Moreover the final assault was still some way off, as, unknown to the defenders, the French had built a complete second line behind their broken front line. The second line, too, had to be bombarded before the launching of a successful assault in which the Battalion suffered a further 198 casualties. The siege had lasted nearly three months when the citadel eventually surrendered in September, and according to General Graham, 'Our ultimate success depended on the repeated attacks made by The Royal Scots'. 'St Sebastian' remains one of the Regiment's proudest honours.

Despite its losses the 3rd Battalion was given no rest, immediately joining the advance on Bayonne and being the first unit of the army to cross into France. In the battle on the River Nivelle the Battalion was only lightly engaged, but it played a larger part in the two-day action on the River Nive, for which it was awarded the honour 'Nive', Sir John Hope, commander of the left wing of the army, reporting, 'Both on the 10th and 11th the good conduct of The Royals was particularly deserving of commendation'. The Battalion then stayed on near Bayonne as part of the army which, by February of 1814, had completely invested the city. A last action, against a French counterattack, was fought on 14 April, Napoleon having in fact abdicated two days before. By September the Battalion was back in Ireland, the last British troops to leave France, their service since 1810 summed up in the regimental honour 'Peninsula'.

One final effort remained for the 3rd Battalion. On Napoleon's escape from Elba it was sent to Belgium, where it formed part of Pack's brigade in the 5th Division under Picton. The Battalion was by now mostly composed of young soldiers, as the experienced veterans of the Peninsular War had nearly all been discharged at the end of 1814, but it was nevertheless rushed into action as soon as the French were engaged. On 16 June, after a hot, dusty, 21-mile march the Battalion reached Quatre Bras, where they immediately charged and routed a French column. The fighting that followed was well described by an officer present at the scene: 'After being engaged for some time in line, the Battalion was formed into square to resist the enemy's cavalry, who were then advancing in great force, and I have the pride of stating that though charged for six or seven times by an infinite superiority of numbers, the French cavalry never for an instant made the slightest impression upon the square of The Royal Scots.' Although they gave no ground all day the Battalion did suffer very heavy casualties from artillery and from skirmishers who crept close in the high corn.

The Battle of Waterloo followed two days later, on the 18th. After a night of torrential rain the much depleted Royals took their place in the 700-yard front held by Picton's Division. The Division, only 3,000 strong, bore the brunt of the first French infantry attack by a corps of 13,000, which was beaten off in confusion. Thereafter the course of the battle is well known, but one incident stood out for The Royals. Four officers in succession had fallen carrying the King's Colour. On the death of the last, Ensign Kennedy, a sergeant tried to take the colour in turn. However, the dead man's grip could not be loosened so the sergeant, undaunted, picked up man and colour and carried both back to the British lines. Chivalrously the Colonel commanding the nearest French troops restrained his men from firing until the sergeant was safe.

The Battles of Quatre Bras and Waterloo cost the 3rd Battalion 363 casualties out of a strength of 624. Douglas relates how on the 19th, 'out of a company 100 strong on the morning of the 16th eleven now sat round to drink, not the health, but the memory of those who had vacated their places in the ranks'. The honour 'Waterloo' was not lightly earned. The Battalion, however, only survived the battle by two years. It first moved to Paris where it formed part of the Army of Occupation, and then in 1817 it crossed to England where it was disbanded in April. The Regiment was reduced to two battalions again, and its regular strength was to remain at that for the rest of the century.

Chapter 5

A FTER Waterloo the first half of the nineteenth century was marked for both battalions of the Regiment by a great number of moves. What action there was before the Crimean War, however, was confined entirely to the 2nd Battalion, the 1st Battalion having a remarkably quiet time. While the 3rd Battalion was fighting at Waterloo the 1st was on its way home from Canada. The following year, 1816, it was posted to Ireland, and there it remained until 1825 when it sailed for the West Indies. On arrival the Battalion was split into detachments and remained so until it returned to Ireland in 1836. By that time it was beginning to recover from the effects of the Napoleonic Wars in that there were 305 Scots to 83 English and 289 Irish. It only spent two years in Ireland before moving again. Between the years 1838 and 1851 it visited in turn Scotland, Gibraltar, the West Indies, Nova Scotia and New Brunswick, and England. In England it remained until posted to the Crimea. Little of importance occurred during this period. Most noteworthy perhaps is that the title of the Regiment was changed in 1821 back to the old style of The First or The Royal Regiment of Foot, instead of The First Regiment of Foot, The Royal Scots, which had prevailed since 1812. By this time the Marquess of Huntly, later Duke of Gordon, was colonel, having succeeded HRH the Duke of Kent in 1820. The Duke of Gordon was succeeded in turn, in 1834, by Lord Lynedoch, formerly Sir Thomas Graham, the divisional commander in the Peninsula.

Such changes were probably of rather less significance to the 2nd Battalion as it was generally much more active during the period. In India fighting in earnest began for the Battalion in 1817, shortly after it had ceased, for the time being, in Europe. In that year the Mahratta War broke out, and the British forces were formed into two Divisions. The two light companies were detached with the 1st Division, but the rest of the Battalion joined the 2nd Division near Nagpore, after marching 230 miles in 12 days.

At Nagpore the Battalion, being the only British force present, was split up among the brigades. The Division first routed a force of over 20,000 of the enemy and then besieged the city. After breaches had been made, two attacks were launched simultaneously, involving three companies of the Battalion. One attack failed and the other was withdrawn after suffering very heavy losses, but the following day the city surrendered. The action brought the award of the honour 'Nagpore', which is unique among British regiments.

Meanwhile the 1st Division had engaged the army of Mulhar Rao Holkar before Maheidpoor. There the two light companies of The Royals took part in a highly successful bayonet attack on the enemy centre. The artillery was captured and the attack culminated in the rout of Holkar's army. 'Maheidpoor' was granted as a regimental honour and the Commander-in-Chief's despatch read, 'The undaunted heroism displayed by the Flank Companies of The Royal Scots in storming and carrying at the point of the bayonet the enemy's guns . . . was worthy of the high name and reputation of that Regiment.'

Most of the rest of the war was spent in minor actions, usually involving the long forced marches so familiar to the Battalion. On one occasion, chasing some 20,000 cavalry, the 2nd Division covered 72 miles in two days, and then made 41 marches in 40 days. In another action at the fort of Talnere a party was ambushed while arranging surrender terms. Major Gordon and Captain Macgregor of The Royals were killed, but the act of treachery so incensed the grenadier company that it assaulted the place and killed the entire garrison. The campaign finally culminated in 1819 with the siege and capture, by the 2nd Division, of Asseerghur, known as 'the Gibraltar of the East', and the following year the Battalion was re-united and posted to Trichinopoly.

In 1825, after three and a half years at Trichinopoly, the

Battalion moved to Rangoon for the war against Burma, which had started the previous year. For most of the campaign the Battalion was split up into detachments of varied and varying size. One detachment of 50 men went up the Irrawaddy in what must have been one of the earliest steamboats in existence. The Burmese continually threw up stockaded works, and a large part of the fighting consisted of storming these. Ultimately the war was successfully concluded when the Burmese were brought to open battle at Pagan-Myo, near their capital, the name of which, 'Ava', commemorates the campaign on the regimental colour.

The climate and terrain in the Burmese campaign were particularly unpleasant, and the British losses from disease were almost equal to the entire original force. The Battalion alone lost 428 from disease. Its next posting was to Bangalore and this afforded some chance for recuperation as it remained there till it sailed for home in 1831. However, an indication of the severity of Indian service at that time is given by the fact that of the Battalion that had originally sailed for India a solitary private returned, and he died within the year.

The climate, if the most fatal, was not the only problem with which the Battalion had to contend. Although always as fit as possible for active service, with good discipline and a high standard of training, The Royal Scots, along with all the other British troops, suffered from a disgraceful supply situation. In 1824 they 'had greatcoats, but they were purchased by the men.' In 1829 'the belts, which have been returned as unfit for service for the last six years, would not now carry the men's ammunition one march from Bangalore.' The prize money for the Mahratta War of 1817–19 was not received until 1831, by which time, of course, most of those who had fought in the war were dead. It was not surprising that the 2nd Battalion arrived in Scotland in 1832 with clothing, arms and equipment all barely serviceable.

The low standard of arms and equipment was, however, not a problem confined to India. The condition of the 1st Battalion on leaving for the West Indies in 1825 is reported to have been just as poor. This state of affairs was due primarily to the usual reaction against military expenditure on the conclusion of a war. Although uniform provided a contrast to the peculiar 'economy' in other spheres in that it became more expensive, it showed a similar lack of touch with the military realities by also becoming more ornate and impractical. The tails of the red coat were lengthened, and it was worn over grey-blue trousers strapped under the boot. The shako widened to a flat top and was particularly unwieldy, but in 1829 it was simplified to something like a peaked top hat. That year also saw a great reduction in ornamentation, the introduction of black trousers with a red stripe, and an improvement in the pack, but the uniform still remained much too tight, and considerably less practical than, for instance, that worn in the Peninsula.

In addition to such problems the 2nd Battalion suffered from the frequency and length of its postings abroad. After its twenty-four years in India the Battalion had only four years in Scotland and Ireland before being posted to Canada in 1836. At the time the Battalion was only 520 strong, and possibly for this reason it was the subject of yet another experiment in economy, this time conducted by the Admiralty. It was decided to try transporting a battalion in a single large ship instead of several small ones. By the time the whole Battalion, including women and children, had crowded into the selected ship, an old East Indiaman, there was standing room only on the decks and several men were hanging on outside. After an inspection by the GOC, Cork District, during which his staff officer fainted, 120 men were ordered ashore, but the ship was still very overcrowded and also verminous. Nevertheless on landing at Quebec the Battalion was commended for its smart appearance.

Towards the end of 1837, after the Battalion had been in Canada for about a year, a series of rebellions broke out around Montreal. While engaged in suppressing these the Battalion assaulted the towns of St Charles and St Eustache, capturing them only after most of the predominantly wooden buildings had been set on fire during the street-fighting. The rest of the Canadian posting was quite uneventful and in November, 1843, the Battalion sailed for the West Indies.

The right wing of the Battalion and HQ sailed aboard the transport *Premier*, but they had not gone beyond the Gulf of St Lawrence before the ship struck a rock in the early hours of the morning. Nothing could be done until daylight, but despite the obvious danger of the ship breaking up in the heavy seas discipline remained extremely firm. In the morning a line was taken ashore and with the help of some French Canadians everybody was ferried to safety. Sir Daniel Lysons described how 'the children were tied up five or six together in blankets, like dumplings, and lowered into the boats'. An officer then covered the 300 miles to Quebec in 4 days to summon help and eventually the wing returned to Quebec by steamship. The detachment's conduct was praised by both the Queen and the Duke of Wellington.

As a result of the shipwreck the Battalion was not re-united in Barbados until late 1844. It remained in the West Indies until 1846, when, after a very brief re-union with the 1st Battalion which had just arrived there, it sailed for Scotland. The next seven years were spent in Scotland, England and Ireland, and must have provided a well deserved and much needed breather for the 2nd Battalion before they embarked on another particularly unpleasant campaign, the Crimean War.

In fact the 2nd Battalion did not see action in the Crimea until well after the 1st Battalion. The latter sailed from England early in 1854. Its transport, the SS *Oude*, was as usual overcrowded and ill equipped, and shortly after leaving Gibraltar there was a serious fire. The scene is described by Private John Willis, of the 3rd Company, writing to his wife: 'But about 12-o-clock noon a most alarming fire broke out in the engine room, and raged with violence for about an hour and a half, but by the steady and persevering manner in which our men worked, with God's assistance, it was extinguished. . . . I was greatly alarmed for there was no land near us, and, another thing, we had an immense lot of ammunition on board, but that was the first thing was thrown over.'

The fire was only the first of many troubles. In the same letter, written from Gallipoli, where the Battalion first landed, Private Willis goes on to say: 'Our bedding here would badly agree with you. We have nothing but our gray coat and blanket to sleep on, and we have to carry the blanket on our knapsack along with a little water barrel that's slung over our shoulder and hangs on the left side.' This was only a very minor example of the extremely poor supply and equipment situation from which the entire army suffered.

In other related aspects the war was very harsh on the troops, a most notorious example being the casualty rate from disease. Again Private Willis makes some interesting comments. He starts off by saying, 'There has been an immense lot of our men died here with cholera,' and then, perhaps not surprisingly, remarks, 'We are actually getting tired and low-spirited to see all our fine able comrades lying low beneath the turf, as well as ever tonight and dead in the morning. I may say all the deaths that has taken place were sudden, some only living a few hours. Our regt. has lost 20 for what came of this month and I can safely say there's some regts. has lost over 5 times that much.' In a final comment he sums up the whole situation: 'God help us, I think this country is a regular pesthouse.'

These observations are all the more telling when one considers that the first two quoted were written at Varna, i.e. before the Battalion had even gone into action. From Varna the Battalion took part in the unopposed landing at Kalamita Bay in September, 1854. At the Battle of the Alma which followed shortly afterwards it was in reserve, and though the battle is one of the regimental honours it had only 1 man slightly wounded. Sebastopol was then invested and the Battalion played an important part in the Battle of Inkerman, which checked a Russian counter-attack, though again losses were slight. Battle casualties in fact were minimal, there being only about ten in the five months of the 1854–5 winter, as compared to losses from disease, which now mounted alarmingly, reaching over 300 in the same five months. The situation was not improved by the poor standard of the hospitals, although the arrival of Florence Nightingale reduced the hospital death rate by half, and it was badly aggravated by the shortage of fuel, food, blankets and clothing. As if such problems were not enough the army was additionally handicapped by the incompetence of the command, allied to the generally out-of-date approach to tactics. In his history of the regiment Colonel Simpson mentions a typical, if minor, example of this type of folly: 'A new breastwork had to be built on captured ground very close up to the Russians. The working party piled arms some distance behind where they were to work and went forward unarmed. When attacked they fell back on their arms, unpiled and counter-attacked, then went back and piled arms again. This happened six times in one night.'

All in all the 2nd Battalion was extremely lucky that it did not reach the Crimea until April, 1855. It had in fact sailed from Ireland before the 1st Battalion, in early 1853. However, once again it was shipwrecked, this time in the Ionian Islands. No one was lost, due partially to the fine discipline, for which the Battalion was commended, as before, but the Battalion then removed to the island of Cephalonia. Life in Cephalonia was described by Major-General Bell in his *Rough Notes of an Old Soldier* as 'Parades, drills, dinners, evening-parties, riding and driving, sea-bathing, and dropping bits of silver into the clear blue sea for Greek boys to dive for, always with success.' There the Battalion spent two extremely pleasant years before eventually sailing for the Crimea.

The 2nd Battalion naturally suffered much less from disease than the 1st Battalion as it spent so little time in the field. Surprisingly, however, its battle casualties were somewhat heavier, even though neither Battalion was engaged in the main assaults on Sebastopol in September, their division being in support. Shortly afterwards Sebastopol was evacuated and before the year was out the war had ended. The Regiment gained three battle honours, 'Alma', 'Inkerman' and 'Sevastopol', and also its first VC. This was won by Private Prosser for two distinct acts of gallantry during the Siege of Sevastopol. On one occasion, despite heavy enemy fire, he rescued a wounded man from another regiment who was lying in no-man's-land unable to move. His other effort was 'pursuing and apprehending (while exposed to two cross-fires) a soldier of the 88th Regiment in the act of deserting to the enemy'. Apart from these bright spots, the war is no pleasanter in retrospect than it can have been at the time, and it must have been with great relief that The Royals finally sailed from the Crimea in 1856.

Chapter 6

O N leaving the Crimea in 1856 the 1st Battalion sailed
straight home and was reviewed by the Queen at Aldershot. It was then posted to Dublin where it was feted.
The 2nd Battalion fared less well and made up for its com-
paratively easy Crimean service by sailing first to Malta and
then the following year for Gibraltar. The year after that, 1858,
it was posted to Hong Kong, the first time any part of the
Regiment had served in China.

The bulk of the Battalion remained in Hong Kong throughout
1859 but about a hundred men were detached to take part in
three expeditions that were mounted from Canton. Little resistance was encountered on these expeditions which were
primarily designed to impress the inhabitants of the region with
a display of strength, but the following year the entire Battalion
sailed from Hong Kong and took part in some brisk fighting
around the Taku forts. After taking these the Battalion marched
on Pekin via Tientsin. On the surrender of Pekin the Battalion
returned to Hong Kong and thence sailed for home, the Regiment
being awarded the battle honours 'Taku Forts' and 'Pekin'.

The brief flurry of activity in China was the forerunner to
another of the Regiment's periods of much movement and little
action. The 2nd Battalion served round England until 1863,
moved to the Channel Islands in 1864, Ireland in 1865, and then
in 1866 returned to India where it stayed until 1880. During this
period of Indian service it was mostly divided into detachments
in various different stations, but in 1873 and '74 the Battalion
was united for service at Ranikhet, its first hill station.

At the time the 2nd Battalion was sent to India the 1st
Battalion was already serving there, having been posted out on
account of the Indian Mutiny in 1857. The 1st Battalion was
stationed in Mahratta country and took no part in the suppression

of the Mutiny, remaining on garrison duty until its return home in 1870. The Battalion returned via Suez, though the canal was not yet completed, and then served in England, Scotland and Ireland successively before being posted to Malta in 1878. Due to the outbreak of the Afghan War the 2nd Battalion did not leave India until 1880. It would otherwise have left when the 1st Battalion went to Malta, as by now the system of having one battalion serving abroad and the other at home was accepted usage. In other respects also the Regiment was becoming recognizably more modern. The 1st Battalion had fought in the Crimea with the French Minié rifle, and in 1856 the 2nd Battalion was issued with Enfield rifles. In 1858 the grenadier and light companies were abolished and every company became a similar fighting unit for the first time since the introduction of the bayonet in the early eighteenth century. Dress was increasingly simplified. By 1875 the tunic was very similar to that worn by the Guards today. Trousers were dark blue with a thin red stripe. The peaked shako was much smaller, the glengarry being introduced as a forage cap, and 1880 saw the first appearance of the diced-bordered peaked cap.

In 1881 there were much more striking changes under the Cardwell Reforms. Dress became that of a non-kilted Highland regiment, with Highland doublets and tartan trews. The tartan was a composite one, similar to the Black Watch, and although several applications were made to wear the Hunting Stuart, permission was not granted until the beginning of the next century. The blue helmet, similar to a police helmet and common to most English regiments, was worn until the introduction of the Kilmarnock bonnet in 1903.

The regimental title also was affected. In 1871 the title had been changed from The First or The Royal Regiment of Foot to The First Regiment of Foot, The Royal Scots, the title it had borne from 1812 to 1821. In 1881 the title was changed yet again to The Lothian Regiment (The Royal Scots), in accordance with the new territorial approach. This was felt to so obscure the Regiment's historical associations that the following year, in response to pressure, it was altered again to The Royal Scots (The Lothian Regiment). As a further concession the Regiment was also allowed pipers, which it had not had for many years, although no more than five were permitted and they were not on the establishment, the Regiment having to support them.

Changes in title and uniform were, however, minor, incidental aspects of the Cardwell Reforms, which centred on the abolition of the numerical system of denominating regiments in favour of the territorial system. As the title implied the regimental area under the new system was the Lothian counties, and also Peebles, the militia and volunteer battalions in the area becoming linked to the Regiment. Thus all infantry regiments were established at two-battalion strength, and in the case of The Royal Scots, already having two line battalions, the Queen's Regiment of Light Infantry Militia (founded as the Edinburgh Light Infantry Militia) became its 3rd Battalion. In 1888 a local volunteer unit, the Queen's Edinburgh Rifles, became affiliated to the Regiment as the Queen's Rifle Volunteer Brigade, and other volunteer units followed, being numbered as battalions of the Regiment from the 4th to the 8th, culminating in the formation, in 1900, of the Highland Battalion as a separate, kilted battalion of The Queen's Rifle Volunteer Brigade.

Apart from confirming the system of operating one battalion abroad and the other at home the reforms of 1881 marked a decisive break for the Regiment. It had been founded as a Scottish regiment rather than a specifically Highland or Lowland one. With the expansion of the Empire, the increasing emphasis on colonial service and the resulting drain on manpower, rendered the more acute for The Royal Scots by the formation of the Highland regiments, it had ceased to be exclusively Scottish, and, on occasions, as noted, become predominantly English or Irish. After 1881 the operation of yearly drafts kept soldiers in the Regiment for their entire service, instead of being drafted elsewhere as had often happened when their own battalion returned home from foreign service. As a result the Scottish element in the Regiment was fostered and maintained, and the part-active,

part-reserve system of service kept a pool of trained men con-
stantly at the ready. The militia and volunteer battalions formed
an extra reserve, although they could only be sent abroad if they
volunteered.

As far as the 2nd Battalion was concerned, however, such
reserves were not to be required for many years. After leaving
India in 1880 the Battalion spent ten years in Ireland before
sailing for Malta, where it remained for two years, returning
to India again in 1892. Apart from the years 1895 to 1899, spent
in Burma, with one company mounted, it stayed in India until
1909.

Meanwhile the 1st Battalion was having a much more active
time. The campaign in Egypt from 1882 to 1884 would have
claimed the Battalion's services but for the fact that in 1882
four companies had already left Malta for the West Indies. The
rest of the Battalion therefore followed, and stayed in the West
Indies through 1883 before being ordered to Egypt again in 1884.
On this occasion it was diverted at Gibraltar to South Africa.

This was the first time any part of the Regiment had been
posted to South Africa. The country was soon to become familiar
to the 1st Battalion though, as it saw the Regiment's only active
service in the next 30 years. The Battalion was immediately
sent to Bechuanaland and attached to the Bechuanaland Field
Force to help deal with the Boer raiding parties from the Orange
Free State. Although taking part in several patrolling expeditions
the Battalion saw no action, but the pattern was set for future
campaigns by the emphasis on mobility and speed of movement
and the use of a company of the Battalion as mounted
infantry.

Service with the Bechuanaland Field Force was followed by a
spell at Cape Town, with a detachment at St Helena, from 1885
to 1887. The years 1888 to 1890 were spent in Zululand, which
was somewhat unsettled at the time. Again the chief activity was
patrolling expeditions, and, mobility proving as important as
against the Boer horsemen, the Battalion provided two mounted
companies during this period.

Although returning home immediately after serving in Zululand the 1st Battalion did not have a long respite. In 1899, on the outbreak of the Boer War, the Battalion sailed back to South Africa in November. At this time a battalion on mobilization consisted of about 70 per cent reservists and the occasion was regarded as a test of the new mobilization system. In reply to questions in the Commons the Under-Secretary of State for War announced that 'The Royal Scots is the only regiment in which every reservist is accounted for'. In addition, both the 1st Battalion and other units were strengthened during the war by detachments from the Royal Scots Volunteer Battalions, and the 3rd Battalion, originally sent to Belfast to relieve the 1st Battalion, volunteered for active service abroad and had reached Cape Town by March, 1900.

The 1st Battalion was initially engaged in the protection of communications behind the main advance and was thus involved in only a few skirmishing actions. From the beginning of 1900, however, a mounted infantry section of about a hundred was detached and operated with the main advance on Kimberley, Bloemfontein and Pretoria. By March two more mounted infantry sections had been formed and from April, for a time, the 3rd Battalion was brigaded with the 1st.

It was not until late August that the 1st Battalion joined the main British army, for the last phase of the offensive, when it was attached to the troops under General Ian Hamilton which operated briefly as a detached flanking force before rejoining the rest o fthe army for the final advance east on Komatipoort. The Battalion remained in garrison at Komatipoort for most of October and November, and there performed a duty new to the Regiment. Corporal Howden, who kept a diary throughout the campaign, noted that 'they have been very busy learning some of the soldiers to drive engines as they are very short of engine drivers. Some are very good, others very bad.' From Komatipoort the Battalion moved to Baberton where it protected the railway during the end of 1900 and the early months of 1901. Most of the rest of the war, until a month before peace in May, 1902,

c

was spent on mobile column work and patrolling and raiding expeditions.

The distinguishing feature of the war was the mobility of the Boers. The effect on the Regiment was that, apart from the first formed mounted section which was engaged twenty-eight times on the main advance, it saw little action despite much hard marching. Casualties as a result were slight, the 1st Battalion losing less than 100 men, mostly from typhoid, but the regimental record is nonetheless impressive. The 1st Battalion marched 2,400 miles in 10 months and on one occasion, at the Battle of Paardeberg, the rapidity of its movement drew from Sir Redvers Buller the remark, 'By Jove! those Royal Scots are devils to go.' The 3rd Battalion performed equally well and in fact gained such renown for the speed of its forced marches that its officers and men were referred to as 'the Bloody Greyhounds'.

Moreover the marches, if lacking in action, were by no means unproductive. On one five-day march in the middle of 1901 the 1st Battalion captured 14 prisoners, 38 rifles, 1,785 rounds SAA, 667 cattle, 2,990 sheep, 8 horses, 72 waggons and 17 saddles. Although by this stage the Boers were reduced to guerrilla warfare the mobile nature of the campaign had from the start made possible surprising captures of men and equipment. The war in fact was noted for the frequency with which small British units surrendered when there was apparently little to gain by resistance. The Regiment, therefore, was particularly proud of the fact that there was not a single case of surrender by a Royal Scot during the entire war and it could consider well-earned its honour 'South Africa 1899–1902'.

The 1st Battalion returned home in 1903. By now khaki was the normal training dress, but red remained for walking out and ceremonial occasions. As if by way of an additional recognition of their services the Regiment as a whole was at last granted permission to wear the Hunting Stuart tartan, the Kilmarnock bonnet shortly afterwards replacing the blue helmet. The way had been paved by the Highland Battalion which had worn the Hunting Stuart tartan from 1901. In that year it had split from the Queen's Rifle Volunteer Brigade and become the 9th Volunteer Battalion (Highlanders), The Royal Scots, and such was its sartorial elegance that it rapidly earned for itself the nickname of the 'Dandy Ninth'.

The Highland Battalion, like the other volunteer units, became a territorial battalion in 1907–8. Under the army re-organization of those years the Queen's Rifle Volunteer Brigade became the Regiment's 4th and 5th territorial battalions, while the 4th and 5th became the 6th and 7th, with the 6th and 7th being amalagamated as the 8th. The 9th of course was the Highland and from the 8th was formed the 10th Territorial Cyclist Battalion. However, it was the 3rd (Militia) Battalion which was most affected. It became the 3rd (Special Reserve) Battalion with the task of training and providing re-inforcements for the regular battalions in time of war, a change from the hard marching service it had given in the Boer War.

In 1913 the internal organization of the battalions also was changed. The number of companies was reduced from eight to four and each company was divided into four platoons instead of two half-companies of two sections each. The rifle remained the only company weapon but each battalion was provided with a two-gun machine-gun section. The only other change before 1914 was the regular home and foreign service alternation of the 1st and 2nd Battalions in 1909. Thus organized The Royal Scots entered the Great War with two regular battalions, one at home and one in India, one special reserve and seven volunteer battalions.

Chapter 7

THE outbreak of the First World War in August, 1914, found the British Army capable of rapid mobilization but limited in size, even allowing for the territorials who were intended to be Home Service units anyway. Lord Kitchener's warning of the likely length of the struggle and the numbers that would be required resulted in a vast expansion, and the effect on The Royal Scots was that the number of battalions increased to thirty-five. The first new battalions to be raised were the New Army units, of which The Royal Scots ultimately had seven, numbering from 11 to 17, as well as two garrison battalions. The extra numbers were made up by the expansion of the territorial battalions of the regiment, all of which achieved three line strength. In due course, however, the maintenance of the third line battalions proved too much and all were amalgamated into a 4th Reserve battalion. The 2/5th and 2/6th battalions also disappeared, being absorbed by the 2/4th.

Fifteen Royal Scots battalions served as active front line units: the 1st and 2nd, as regulars, obviously; six New Army battalions, the 11th, 12th, 13th, 15th, 16th and 17th; and the 1st battalions of the territorials, except for the 10th. The 1/10th remained at home but the 2/10th fought in Russia in 1918 and 1919. Of the remainder the 2nd territorial battalions and the New Army's Reserve battalions, the 14th and 18th, remained at home. The 19th was a labour battalion and worked in France in 1917, and the 1st garrison battalion performed near active service at Gallipoli. More than 100,000 men passed through all these battalions, of whom over 11,000 were killed and over 40,000 wounded. The casualty list in fact is estimated as being greater than that of the entire British Army during the Peninsular War. As a measure of the Regiment's services it is only parallelled by the roll of battle honours, of which there were 71, as well as innumerable individual medals and awards, including 6 VCs.

In the initial stages of the war only the regulars were involved. The 2nd Battalion, being in England at the time, formed part of the original British Expeditionary Force and was in action at Mons on 23 August. There the Battalion was only lightly engaged, though the last unit of the 3rd Division to retire, but it saw some fierce fighting at Le Cateau before continuing the retreat. Conditions on the march south were not pleasant, as the country was in the throes of a heatwave at the time, but discipline remained perfect, and in sharp contrast to other units neither greatcoats nor any other equipment was discarded. The Battalion then participated in the counter-attack across the Marne and the Aisne and saw its first trench warfare in September.

After the initial phases of the war the BEF turned towards the coast and engaged in a flanking race against the Germans. The 2nd Battalion was chiefly involved at Neuve Chapelle and La Bassée. It then settled down for the winter at Kemmel and participated successfully in one of the first trench to trench attacks featuring a preliminary bombardment and set, limited objectives. During this action Private H. H. Robson won the Regiment's first VC of the war, rescuing one wounded man and making a gallant bid to rescue another.

In November the 8th Battalion became the first Scottish territorials to reach France. They were so fit that they were almost immediately sent to the front line, as part of the 7th Division. The next territorial battalion was the 9th which arrived in February to join the 27th Division. Meanwhile, however, the 1st Battalion had arrived from India, and though also attached to the 27th Division, met the 2nd Battalion, shortly after its arrival in France, for only the second time since the Crimea.

The first half of 1915 was relatively quiet except on the Ypres Salient. Here in April the 9th Battalion helped in a vital holding action after the line was badly broken by the first gas attack. Until the end of 1917 the Salient remained one of the worst sectors in the line. According to Major Ewing, 'The very name "Ypres" came to signify something evil; it was personified as a malevolent demon with an insatiable passion for human sacrifices.' The 1st Battalion saw some hard service with the 9th in this notorious area while the 2nd was never far from it until the Battle of the Somme in 1916. The 8th Battalion, meanwhile, served mostly near Festubert, also an unpleasant sector at this time. At Givenchy in June Lance-Corporal W. Angus (HLI attached 8th Royal Scots) was awarded the VC after he openly exposed himself to enemy fire, suffering about 40 wounds, in order to rescue a wounded officer. Later in the same month the 8th Battalion was formed into a pioneer unit, a task for which it was particularly well suited as it was composed principally of miners.

By this time the focus of British attention had switched temporarily from France and Flanders to the Dardanelles and the ill-fated Gallipoli campaign. Three Royal Scots battalions were involved in this, the 4th, 5th and 7th, but only the 5th was present at the landing in April, and then only in reserve, as the rest of the 29th Division were regular troops. On 28 April, however, the Battalion suffered heavy losses in the attempt to storm the Achi Baba ridge. The failure of this attack condemned the troops to many months of siege and trench warfare with little likelihood of success. As one officer of the Battalion said, 'We have properly let ourselves in for it.' Nowhere on the peninsula was safe or free from the alarms of war, but the discomfort was rendered far more intense by the 'noisome stench' aroused by the slightest breeze, by dust and sand everywhere, by thirst, an extremely hot sun and flies and mosquitoes 'so densely massed that they appeared to form a wavering shadow round a man's head'. About the only consolation was the proximity of the Mediterranean for bathing and 'a complete wash was the supreme height of luxury that Gallipoli afforded'.

As a result of the losses and setbacks in Gallipoli the 5th Battalion was shortly joined by the 4th and 7th Battalions who arrived with the 52nd Lowland Division in June as part of the reinforcements. The 7th Battalion had lost half its strength before leaving home due to an appalling railway crash near Gretna in which two companies were put out of action and over 200 men of the Battalion killed. The 4th Battalion arrived intact, despite its ship's involvement in a major collision in the Aegean, and shortly after landing relieved the 5th Battalion in the lines. Then, on 28 April, both the 4th and the 7th Battalions, as part of the 156th Brigade, were involved in a major attack which was in due course supported by the 5th Battalion, from reserve, on the right of the 7th. This was the only occasion in the history of the Queen's Edinburgh Rifles when the 4th and 5th Battalions fought together, but it was overshadowed by the appalling losses suffered. The chief objective of the attack was on the left of the 156th Brigade whose targets were not shelled at all. Under the circumstances the 4th and 7th Royal Scots achieved a rare and magnificent feat in carrying all their objectives without artillery support, but the 4th Battalion alone had over 360 casualties.

The attack of 28 June was the last major action at Gallipoli for the 5th Battalion. It was by now reduced to less than company strength and in July embarked for the Island of Mudros for rest and reinforcements. There it was built up to nearly half battalion strength and returned in August for two bouts of trench duty at Suvla Bay before finally leaving Gallipoli in October. The wastage rate of the 4th and 7th Battalions was even higher. Within two weeks the 4th was reduced to 458 men and the two companies of the 7th to 175 men. For the time being, therefore, they were united and performed sterling service as reserve to an attack on 12 July. The composite battalion was divided in September, on the arrival of 12 officers and 440 other ranks for the 7th Battalion, but was re-united in early November because the strength of the 4th had been so reduced by dysentery.

The Royal Scots took part in one more action of note on the peninsula, a remarkably successful surprise raid on 15 November. After August, however, major engagements had ceased and, with the snow and slimy mud of winter replacing the heat, dust and flies of summer, it was obvious that the campaign was a failure. The Royal Scots remained to the end but it was with relief that on 8 January, as rearguard to the 52nd Division, they eventually left Gallipoli for good.

While the 4th, 5th and 7th Royal Scots were fighting in the Dardanelles the first New Army battalions were entering the trenches in France. When the 8th Battalion left Festubert to train as pioneers they were relieved by the 11th Royal Scots who were brigaded with the 12th in the 9th (Scottish) Division. In early August the 13th Battalion also moved into the front line with the 15th (Scottish) Division. By September all three battalions were quite sufficiently battle-hardened to take part in the Loos offensive.

Simultaneously with the Battle of Loos a diversionary attack was launched on the Ypres Salient. The 2nd Battalion played a prominent part in this and secured all its objectives on the morning of the attack (25 September), but in the face of the German counterattack had to retire with the rest of the line to its original positions. The offensive at Loos followed a similar course in that after initial successes the British forces had to face exceptionally strong counterattacks. Thus, though in reserve, the 11th and 12th Battalions at Haisnes and the 13th at Loos all saw extremely heavy defensive fighting during which Private R. Dunsire of the 13th won a VC for his gallant and skilful rescue of two wounded men. The casualty figures alone, 378 in the 11th, 294 in the 12th, and 340 in the 13th, speak for the determination with which these new battalions fought.

After Loos the Western Front settled down for the winter and, with the evacuation of Gallipoli, the only other points at which Royal Scots were engaged were Macedonia and Egypt. After the defeat of Serbia, Macedonia was the allies' last toehold in the Balkans and reinforcements, including the 1st Royal Scots with the 27th Division, were sent out there to the French in December. The Battalion landed at Salonika, where the mud surpassed even that of the Salient, and in January moved to Gomonic in the Laganza valley. There the Battalion stayed until June, but conditions were so quiet that they saw no action at all.

In contrast to Macedonia there was action in Egypt during

the winter and early months of 1916. The 6th Battalion was the first unit of The Royal Scots out there. It had contributed so much of its strength to the 4th and 8th Battalions that it did not leave Scotland until September, when it sailed straight for Egypt. After a period of training at Cairo the Battalion spent December and January in Western Egypt fighting the Senussi tribesmen. The fighting was not intense but the Battalion was engaged in several sharp, minor actions and acquitted itself well. After the defeat of the Senussi in February the Battalion spent two more months in Egypt before sailing in May for the much less pleasant war in France.

While the Senussi campaign was being waged in the West the East of Egypt was being reinforced by units from Gallipoli, among them the 4th and 7th Royal Scots who resumed their separate identities shortly after landing. While guarding the Suez Canal the Battalions experienced their first sandstorm, which filled the air 'like a peasoup fog'. This was only a foretaste of what was to come for in April a Turkish raid caused both Battalions to be sent East to Pelusium. Neither Battalion saw action since by the time of their arrival the Turks had been beaten off, but they gained valuable experience in marching in deep soft sand, blasted by the hot, south wind, the Khamseen, with the temperature often rising to 125 degrees in the shade, and a liquid allowance of one water bottle per man per day. Small wonder that one officer dreamed of a land where a straight line was 'the shortest distance between me and the next pub'.

In contrast to the aridity of Egypt and the Sinai Peninsula it had been a wet spring in France, particularly in March, thus adding to the discomfort of the troops. For the British, however, the situation was at least relatively quiet during the first half of 1916. The great German offensive at Verdun precluded any major effort elsewhere. Thus the 15th, 16th and 17th Royal Scots, who reached France early in the year, had a long period of easy acclimatization. The 5th and 6th Battalions also reached France in the spring, but since it was obvious that Edinburgh could not make good the losses of both Battalions they were combined as the 5th/6th Royal Scots in June.

The calm period of early 1916 ended for many British troops on 1 July with the first infantry attacks in the Battle of the Somme. The battle was a turning point in the history of the war and set a stereotyped pattern for the conduct of offensives for months afterwards: limited objectives, fixed right and left boundaries, exact timing, and a 'creeping' barrage beforehand, which in the case of the Somme lasted for six days. The element of surprise was completely supplanted by the attempt to destroy utterly the enemy's powers of resistance before the infantry attack. If it did not work the attackers suffered terribly. If it did work and they captured their objectives they often suffered even more from counter-attacks and shell fire. The horrors of the battle surpassed anything that had gone before and were summed up in the words of a veteran soldier of the 12th Battalion: 'You don't know what war is until you have been in the Somme.'

Only two Royal Scots Battalions, the 15th and 16th, were involved in the initial phases of the battle. As part of the 34th Division they attacked together the formidable fortifications of Heligoland, Scots Redoubt and Wood Alley, near the village of La Boisselle. After taking these points, despite a heavy cross-fire from La Boisselle, The Royal Scots held them until the night of the 3rd when they were relieved. By that time their reputation was more than established, but at a cost to the 15th of 628 casualties, and to the 16th of 482. As they were withdrawn the 11th and 12th Battalions were moving into action further south near Montauban. On 14 July both Battalions took part in an attack on the village of Longueval, with the 2nd Battalion moving up on their left. The first stage of the attack was carried out very skilfully and successfully, but the second phase, the capture of the village itself, met with very strong opposition, and eventually became bogged down in costly street fighting. When the 11th and 12th Royal Scots were relieved on the 17th they had lost 321 and 317 men respectively. The 2nd Battalion suffered less, being engaged on trench duty after the initial attack, but even so lost 176.

After the fighting at Longueval an attempt was made to straighten the salient thus created. The 2nd Battalion participated in the attack on Guillemont on the right, while the 9th and then the 15th and 16th were engaged in the fearsome High Wood sector on the left. The 9th in particular suffered there; in one attack by B and C Companies all the officers were hit and only a handful of men returned. The 8th Battalion, as pioneers, suffered only from shellfire, but in one period of twenty-four hours had 100 casualties from this source. The 13th Battalion was far more fortunate. Taking part in the attack on 15 September, it successfully took the village of Martinpuich, beyond its original objective, with less than 300 casualties. This attack saw the first use of tanks, and partially for that reason was generally very successful, though none arrived at Martinpuich until after the village had been taken.

By October the Somme offensive had become bogged down in mud, the 11th and 12th Battalions meeting particularly bad conditions in the Butte de Warlencourt sector. With the drier weather in November the centre of action moved west to the Ancre. By that time the 8th, 9th, 15th and 16th Royal Scots had 'holidayed' at Armentières, 'associated not so much with work as with happy and pleasant times'. The former two Battalions, together with the 5th/6th and 2nd, were involved at Ancre, but only the 2nd saw heavy action, during the unsuccessful assault on Serre. The 2nd Battalion compensated somewhat for this failure with a very successful raid in January, but otherwise the winter was mostly quiet for The Royal Scots in France.

In Macedonia, however, the 1st Royal Scots was at last seeing action. The Battalion moved to the Struma Valley in June and, events having been precipitated by Rumania's entry into the war in August, took a prominent part in the well executed and successful attacks on the villages of Bala and Zir at the end of September. Brigadier-General Widdrington describes visiting Lieutenant-Colonel Forbes of The Royal Scots in Zir shortly afterwards; 'He told me that the Bulgars were still quite close and that they could be heard talking and shouting, which was true enough. I asked why they did not shoot and he replied, "They do," and just then a volley crashed out from quite close. It appeared to amuse The Royal Scots, so I had to pretend that I liked it too, but found urgent business elsewhere.'

The British forces then moved down to the plain, the Battalion taking and holding the village of Homondos for the winter. The next summer saw a retreat to the hills for health reasons and the Battalion had to be content with sport and raiding their old haunts at Homondos. The other Eastern theatre, the Sinai Peninsula, also saw a lull in activity in the summer of 1917, but under very different conditions.

In August, 1916, the Turks had been lured into a trap at Romani, about 20 miles east of the Suez Canal. After their defeat there, in which the 4th and 7th Battalions participated, Egypt was safe from attack and the British could advance towards Palestine. In October the trek east started. The 156th Brigade, at the head of the 52nd Division, did not have the benefit of the wire netting roads laid behind them. The march consequently was very exacting, the foot sinking to the ankle at each step and kicking up a cloud of fine sand, described by one man as 'a form of Turkish bath which ought to be reserved for sybarites in the world of the damned'.

On 22 December the 156th Brigade entered El Arish and Palestine. The next major problem was Gaza. Apart from its naturally commanding site, well supported by man-made fortifications, the city posed a special obstacle in the form of cactus hedges, far more efficient than barbed wire, which interlaced the fertile strip round the city. As a Royal Scots officer put it, 'We never expected war to be a bed of roses, but we did not bargain for it being a bed of cactus hedges.' Not surprisingly Gaza did not fall easily. After the first assault in March had failed, a more deliberate set-piece attack was launched on 19 April. This too was repulsed, but the Royal Scots Battalions were not heavily engaged and had relatively light casualties. A frontal attack was obviously doomed to failure, so while a flanking attack was launched on Beersheba, a holding force, including The Royal Scots Battalions, was left in front of Gaza, to be tormented by the heat, the sand, the flies and, of course, the Turks.

On the Western Front also the Allies were on the offensive in 1917. The Germans had retreated to the Hindenburg Line during the winter and British morale was high. In the Arras sector, where the first attack was launched, this was particularly so; the troops had gained considerably in efficiency over the winter, at least partially due to the fresh emphasis on the use of the rifle, while the grenade, which had enjoyed a vogue in the early years of the war, was relegated to a subordinate place.

Whatever the causes the Arras offensive, which was launched on 9 April, was initially extremely successful. The 2nd, 8th, 9th, 11th, 12th, 13th, 15th, and 16th Royal Scots were all involved in the battle. All obtained their objectives. The 9th Battalion found the enemy trenches so battered as to be indistinguishable from the craters. There was still opposition though, and among the wounded was Captain James Murray of the 12th Battalion. This officer had countered the German Hymn of Hate by composing a Catechism of Blood in which he chanted the questions while his company shouted the responses. Wounded in the first phase of the advance, he carried on and had his hand mangled by a machine-gun bullet. Undeterred, he shot away the dangling skin and bone with his revolver and continued until finally brought down by a wound in the groin. He then insisted that his stretcher-bearers rescue all his men before attending to him. Despite his very severe wounds, he recovered after a long spell in hospital.

9 April, 1917, was one of the most successful days of the war for the British. By the 14th all their objectives had been gained. Unfortunately the French offensive demanded that the pressure be maintained on the Arras front, despite the stiffened German front line. As a result there was some very hard fighting but only limited gains. The 9th Royal Scots took part in the attack near Roeux on the 23rd, described as 'perhaps the most savage

infantry battle that the Division (the 51st) took part in', and naturally had heavy losses. The 13th Battalion also suffered major losses at this stage, while the 15th and 16th Battalions, advancing too deeply relative to their flanks, had casualties of over three-quarters and half of their numbers respectively.

The French offensive of 1917 not only prolonged the Battle of Arras but also caused the opening of the Passchendaele offensive in Flanders to be postponed until 31 July. At first it seemed as if the attack would be as successful as that on the Messines Ridge earlier (which had not involved any Royal Scots units), but the strength of the German counterattacks dispelled this illusion and with the onset of wet weather the offensive was doomed. The 9th and 13th Battalions, operating from Ypres, were involved in the first phase of the attack, but like the rest of the attacking forces soon became bogged down in mud, suffering heavy casualties in conditions of appalling discomfort. A brief spell of dry weather in September saw the resumption of the offensive, the 2nd, 9th, 11th and 12th Royal Scots being engaged. During the initial advances Captain H. Reynolds of the 12th earned a VC when he personally attacked a pill-box, captured the occupants and, though wounded, continued to lead his men to their objective in the face of very heavy fire. Unfortunately the rain soon set in again and the attack squelched to a halt, but not before the 15th and 16th Battalions, fresh from the successful if minor action at Hargicourt, had been severely cut down trying to beat the slime and the Germans.

Cambrai, the last offensive of 1917, provided a distinct contrast to Passchendaele. Launched as a surprise attack on 20 November, it employed heavy concentrations of tanks for the first time. The British, however, were almost as much surprised by the ease and extent of their success as the Germans and the advance was not followed up as much as it might have been, although there were large gains of territory, supplies and prisoners. The 9th Battalion distinguished itself round Fontaine, while the 8th, the only other Royal Scots Battalion involved, performed its usual sterling work, on one occasion wiring the whole Divisional front in a night.

If even the Battle of Cambrai was not particularly satisfactory, at least events in the East provided one bright spot towards the end of 1917. In November Gaza finally fell. If the chief cause of the Turkish retreat was the supposedly impossible flanking attack through Beersheba, the forces in front of Gaza had played a crucial part in holding the Turks' attention. To this end a major attack was launched on 2 November, when the 4th Battalion received the praise of Brigadier-General Leggett for its magnificent feat in capturing the formidable El Arish redoubt and its associated 'Little Devil' trench system.

From Gaza the 4th and 7th Royal Scots moved north through Palestine with the rest of the British forces. Both Battalions fought a skilful action at Burkah and Brown Hill and then, after a severe march inland with worn-out footwear, over a very rough mountain road, were engaged in the heavy fighting on the Nebi Samwil ridge, the key to Jerusalem. On being relieved at Nebi Samwil The Royal Scots started the march back to the coast but were diverted on the way to help deal with a sudden Turkish counterattack on the British flank. After reaching the coast in early December The Royal Scots were posted near the orange groves of Jaffa, on the River Auja, virtually unfordable and apparently a formidable obstacle to further progress. On the night of 20/21 December, however, a remarkable surprise crossing was affected at several points simultaneously. The Turks were taken completely by surprise and The Royal Scots met almost no opposition. Even after driving the enemy beyond artillery range of the bridges the two Battalions had only twenty-nine casualties between them. With this very satisfactory action The Royal Scots' active service in the East ended for, after a three-month rest, in early April they sailed for France, where the war had entered its most critical phase.

On 21 March, 1918, 'the most formidable offensive in the history of the world' broke upon the awaiting allied forces. The German attack was launched on two fronts: against the Fifth

Army which contained the 9th (now in the 61st Division), 11th and 12th Royal Scots, and against the Third Army which contained the 2nd, 8th, 13th, 15th and 16th. All these Battalions, as also the 17th which formed part of the reinforcements for the Fifth Army, were involved in the desperate defence against the German onslaught, and of them all only the 2nd and 17th could not be described as having seen extremely severe action. Inevitably the action was too muddled and scrappy for it to be possible to describe each battalion's tasks and achievements. Certain points, however, stand out, as, for instance, the 11th and 12th Battalion's seven successive days and nights of fighting which cost over 400 casualties in each Battalion. There was also the 100-strong detachment of the 9th Royal Scots which, covering the withdrawal of the 20th Division, 'successfully held the enemy at bay from early morning until 6 pm, when the eleven survivors withdrew under orders, having accomplished their task.' The 9th Battalion then formed a composite battalion with Argylls and Gordons out of the remnants of its brigade. The 8th Battalion discarded its picks and shovels on the retreat from Cambrai and showed that it was just as skilful with rifles, while the 13th Royal Scots, defending Arras, suffered a terrible bombardment, followed by an attack in which the HQ staff saved the line and, having nearly 400 casualties, was reduced to company strength.

By the beginning of April the offensive had petered out in a situation satisfactory to neither side. The main German effort then switched to the River Lys in the area of Béthune and Armentières. The battalions involved in the defence against this attack were the 2nd, 8th, 9th, 11th, 12th, 15th, and 16th, but again it is not possible to distinguish each battalion's contribution to the fighting. Particularly noteworthy, though, was the 12th Battalion's defence of the area round Kemmel when in six days their casualties amounted to nearly 600. The 15th and 16th Battalions also distinguished themselves in some very confused fighting on the River Lys and then on the retreat to Bailleul. There are no figures for the casualties of the 15th Battalion, but the 16th's speak for themselves: 21 officers were killed, wounded

9. *The 12th Royal Scots manning a mine crater at Meteren, 23 June, 1918.*

10. *Lewis gunners of the 12th Battalion, wearing box respirators, in action during a gas attack on 25 June, 1918.*

11. An advanced post of the 1st Royal Scots enduring wintry conditions at Lacelles in January, 1940.

12. Royal Scots celebrating St Andrew's Day in the traditional manner at Pinwe after the occupying Japanese forces had been wiped out.

13. Men of the 1st Battalion with a captured Japanese flag in Burma, 1944.

14. A lone Royal Scots Piper in the Radfan, Aden, 1964.

15. The Princess Royal, Colonel-in-Chief for nearly fifty years, inspecting a Royal Scots Guard of Honour at Dreghorn.

and missing, and 554 other ranks out of a total complement of 785. The 15th cannot have suffered much less, and consequently the action proved to be the last for these fine units, for their losses could not be made up and, after a period of training American reinforcements, both Battalions were disbanded in July.

By that time most of the other Battalions had had a period of rest. The Germans ignored the British forces during May and June and concentrated on the French in the Chemin des Dames sector. For The Royal Scots the period was only noteworthy for the raiding parties conducted by the 2nd, 5th/6th and 13th Battalions and for the arrival of the 4th and 7th Battalions from Palestine.

The 4th and 7th Battalions remained with the 52nd Division in France and were therefore not involved in the first phase of the counter-offensive. This was launched in the French sector and succeeded in throwing the Germans back across the Marne. Three Royal Scots Battalions were involved, the 8th, 9th and 13th, as part of the four British Divisions assisting the French. The 8th Battalion, with the 51st Division, was engaged in the attack on the eastern angle of the German salient that lay between Soissons and Rheims. The Battalion saw some stiff fighting in the Bois de Coutron during the last days of July and suffered particularly from gas. Once the Germans had started to retreat, however, normal pioneer work was resumed and by August the Battalion was back at Arras.

While the 8th Battalion was fighting in the eastern angle of the German salient the 9th and 13th Battalions moved into the trenches in the western angle in the wake of the first attack. Although the western side saw much heavier pressure by the Allies The Royal Scots were not involved in a major attack until 1 August. The 13th Battalion was then only lightly involved, in a successful but purely diversionary raid in the north. The 9th Battalion by contrast suffered very severely. The preliminary barrage was ineffective and support from the French troops to the battalion's right very poor. A frontal assault on well-entrenched positions under such circumstances was doomed to failure and the 9th Battalion lost 80 per cent of its strength in valiantly attacking as ordered. Its efforts, however, were not fruitless for the enemy were put under such pressure that by the following morning they were in full retreat. Along with the rest of the 15th Division, they had so impressed the French that a monument was erected on the highest point of the Buzancy Plateau bearing the inscription, 'Here the thistles of Scotland will bloom for ever among the roses of France'.

The success of the French offensive was the signal for the launching, on 8 August, of the British offensive against Amiens. Only one battalion of The Royal Scots, the 5th/6th, was involved in the main attack, and then only very briefly. On 18 August the 11th Battalion, supported by the 12th, took part in a very successful subsidiary operation, the surprise storming of the Hoegenacker Ridge. The Germans were by now very much on the defensive and there was no point in their hanging onto the Lys salient. By the 22nd they had begun to retreat.

With the failure of their massive effort in the Spring, German morale had slumped dramatically. In the action on the Hoegenacker Ridge the enemy's resistance was minimal. The Ridge was taken at a run, nearly 300 prisoners were captured by The Royal Scots alone and no sort of a counterattack was launched. Such successes were to become more and more frequent as the enemy steadily lost heart. In the words of Major Ewing, 'German confidence, which was a rock in 1916 and 1917, was, in 1918, a wretched cockle boat tossing about rudderless amid waves of disaster which finally engulfed it.'

The next phase of the advance showed the German collapse only too well. The 5th/6th Battalion's advance on 28 August was described as a 'procession' and the Battalion was able to make some 5 or 6 miles in three days. Pulled out of the front line just as it reached the Somme Canal on 30 August the Battalion returned to cross the Canal with ease on 5 September. The enemy thereupon retreated rapidly to the Hindenburg Line and the 5th/6th Battalion saw no more action that month.

The 2nd Battalion, meanwhile, after participating in preliminary operations to clear the Ancre valley and the Arras–Albert railway advanced from the railway. Initially the Battalion's progress was as easy as that of the 5/6th Battalion. This was in large part due to the actions of 'C' Company's runner, Private H. McIver, who won a VC for the extraordinary feat of pursuing a single German 150 yards into a machine-gun nest, killing 6 of the defenders and then capturing 20 prisoners as well as 2 machine-guns, thus 'converting a potential resistance into a rout'. Thereafter the 2nd Battalion met much stiffer resistance. At the village of Noreuil an attempt to assault a coverless ridge was baulked by heavy machine-gun fire and there followed severe trench fighting during which Private McIver was killed. The Battalion was then pulled out of the line and did not return until mid-September when it was again heavily engaged as the Germans launched a surprisingly determined assault on the British positions east of the Somme. That these positions were maintained was due in large part to The Royal Scots' dogged defence of their trenches north of Havrincourt.

Apart from the 8th Battalion, performing their usual sterling work around Fampoux, the only other Royal Scots battalions involved in this phase of the offensive were the 4th and 7th. These had a much easier time than the 2nd Battalion. After a relatively peaceful sojourn on Vimy Ridge they moved into the attack north of the Cojeul River advancing steadily eastwards until they reached the outer defences of the Hindenburg Line. After a brief pause they moved on in early September against the Queant end of the tremendously strong and well-fortified Drocourt-Queant Switch and took their objectives with amazing ease. Both Battalions were then rested until mid-September when they moved into the line near Moeuvres where they met stiffer resistance, including the heaviest shelling either battalion was to encounter in France.

None of the remaining Royal Scots battalions in France were engaged in any major offensive during August and early September, 1918. The 9th and 13th Battalions, however, had an unpleasant time at Mazingarbe in the Loos sector. A policy of 'peaceful penetration' was in operation in this area, which meant that the enemy's positions were to be continually tested and he was to be 'encouraged' to retire by means of raiding parties and minor assaults. There were no 'set' battles, minimal or non-existent artillery bombardments and the whole business was untrumpeted and thoroughly nerve-racking.

By the end of September, fortunately, this type of activity ceased as the allies began their final thrust. By that time the war had already ended for the 1st Battalion in Macedonia. After three month's training the Battalion moved to the Vardar front with the 27th Division in July. The main offensive against the Bulgarians was launched elsewhere, but the 27th Division spent most of September deceiving the enemy into believing that the Vardar sector was the point of attack. The Royal Scots played their full part in this operation, being heavily shelled for their pains. They were rewarded by the enemy's withdrawal from the Vardar front on the 22nd, necessitated by his reverses elsewhere.

The 1st Royal Scots were to see no more fighting, for Bulgaria capitulated on 1 October. Those fit enough were kept hard at work mending the roads, but by then the Battalion's numbers were so reduced by malaria that with the other units of the 81st Brigade they were briefly formed into a composite battalion. The battalions resumed their separate identities in time to march on Turkey in mid-October but that country's capitulation cut short their march and with it their last prospect of hostilities.

In the West, meanwhile, in an attempt to end the war before the winter, the allies launched an offensive on 26 and 27 September along their entire front from the Alps to the sea. The success of this massive operation depended on the British forces in the centre who had to attack the main Hindenburg Line. Whatever the state of the enemy's morale this was a formidable obstacle, particularly for the 4th Army, including the 5th/6th Royal Scots, who faced the strongest sector of all on the St Quentin Canal. The 5th/6th Battalion did not in fact go into action until 1

October. Although by that time the main Hindenburg Line had been breached The Royal Scots were directed to attack perhaps the key position in the secondary line of defences, the village of Sequehart, just north of St Quentin. Its importance was underlined by the determination of the German counterattacks. The village changed hands four times before, on the 3rd, after having specifically requested Sequehart as its objective, the Battalion finally captured the village and held it, despite very heavy shelling and two more fierce counterattacks.

By comparison the other Royal Scots involved in the attack against the Hindenburg Line had a much easier time. The 2nd Battalion, advancing from near its previous position north of Havrincourt, moved so fast that it found itself being attacked from behind by enemy troops it had overrun. This resistance soon collapsed though, and 260 men and seven officers surrendered to 'C' Company alone, with a total complement of less than 100.

The 4th Royal Scots (the 7th was in reserve) was equally successful. Faced with a very well fortified section of the Hindenburg Line on the Canal du Nord a minor flanking attack proved sufficient to destroy the resistance of a demoralized defence and the Battalion gained all its objectives with quite remarkable ease considering the strength of the enemy positions.

The collapse of German spirit was displayed to just as great an extent in Flanders. There, on the 28th, the 11th and 12th Battalions were able to move out of Ypres on the infamous Menin road without even suffering from shellfire. Detailed to attack Becelaere The Royal Scots were briefly held up by an enemy battery but found the German infantry 'little more than spectators' who could be driven 'like sheep'. In fact neither Battalion met serious opposition until early October. The 17th Battalion encountered rather stiffer resistance and brought in few prisoners but nonetheless made substantial advances.

With the resumption of the offensive in Flanders in mid-October all three Battalions were again engaged. The 17th, advancing south of Courtrai, had the easier task this time. After less than a week it had almost ceased to fight. The 11th and 12th Royal Scots on the other hand met trouble north of Courtrai. Two machine-gun posts threatened to hold up the advance at an early stage and they were only subdued as a result of the inspired action of Corporal R. E. Elcock, for which he was awarded the VC. The River Lys formed the next obstacle and in the face of a surprisingly determined defence The Royal Scots were unable to establish a secure bridgehead before being pulled out of the front line. They returned, however, in time for the advance eastwards after the passage of the Lys had been forced, and saw some fierce action on Hill 50 above the village of Vichte before being pulled out of action for good on 24 October.

By now the Germans were so thoroughly disheartened that those Royal Scots battalions still involved rarely met any significant resistance. The 9th Royal Scots, after a brief, very successful action on the Deule Canal, were still pursuing the enemy through Antoing at the Armistice, but the 13th Battalion had by then already spent some time repairing the roads. This, of course, was the 8th Battalion's main job at this time, and was performed as efficiently as usual: when 'B' Company was repairing the Valenciennes road, 'One job was estimated by the Corps as likely to take the Company nine days; it was done in three.'

Of course there were still isolated pockets of resistance. The 2nd Battalion, for instance, underwent a heavy gas attack at Vertain, east of Cambrai, and then, regrettably, suffered even more severely when the supporting barrage fell in the assembly trenches. The German machine-gunners, moreover, maintained their reputation for tenacity until the end and in particular posed problems for the 5th/6th Battalion on the Sambre Canal north of Etreux. They also held up the advance near Hoogmolen in late October, and there Lieutenant D. S. McGregor of the 6th Battalion, attached to the Machine-Gun Corps, was awarded the VC for the brilliant feat of galloping his guns over 600 yards of open road, under heavy fire, in order to engage the enemy effectively. Unfortunately this very gallant officer was killed shortly afterwards while directing mortar fire.

The experiences of the 4th and 7th Battalions were more typical, however. Their march through the country north of Douai and the Conde Canal resembled a triumphal procession rather than an advance. Opposition was only encountered once. On 10 November a solitary shell near the village of Herchies wounded three men of the 7th Battalion and killed one. For The Royal Scots in France it was the last incident of the war. The following day the Armistice was signed.

Chapter 8

No account of The Royal Scots in the First World War would be complete without a mention of the Home Service Battalions. It should be appreciated that these units had a continually shifting personnel as the training staff consisted primarily of officers and men waiting to return to the Front after recovering from wounds. While their chief task was obviously the training and preparation of drafts for the Front they also performed coastal guard duties and tours of Ireland. Both their movements and the drafts they found are too numerous to detail but their overall contribution was summed up by Major Ewing: 'The most convincing testimony to the value of the work performed by the draft-finding units was the magnificent war record of the Active Service Battalions.'

In addition to the Home Service and Active Service Units there were two battalions which served abroad in special capacities. The 19th Battalion was formed in 1917 to serve in France as a labour battalion. The men were below the normal service standard, in many cases because of war wounds, and the work was generally boring. Nevertheless the Battalion was praised because it 'was particularly clean and worked so well that they helped to turn out the largest amount of work of any area in France.'

The 1st Garrison Battalion was formed in 1915 and sent to Mudros, arriving there in November, to relieve troops fit for the front line. The Battalion itself was composed of men designated as unfit for active service but a party of 400 was nevertheless sent on to Cape Helles despite all the protests of Colonel Brown. The remainder were then employed chiefly as a labour battalion, again in the face of Colonel Brown's representations that they were neither suited nor intended for that work. Not until Cape Helles was evacuated was the Battalion re-united. It then moved to Alexandria where it formed part of the defence system. Finally, towards the end of 1916, the first drafts of the Battalion moved to Cyprus. There The Royal Scots' chief job was guarding prisoners, a task which, despite understaffing, they performed as conscientiously as they had all others, until they eventually sailed for home and disbandment in May, 1919.

One other Royal Scots battalion saw foreign service, in its case active service. The 2/10th Battalion was originally recruited in under a week in September, 1914. After the arrival of uniforms and equipment in January, 1915, the Battalion was based on Berwick. A cyclist battalion, it was responsible for a share of East Coast defence as well as providing drafts for overseas service. In June, 1918, the Battalion moved to Ireland where it remained for just over a month. By that time many of the men were classified 'B1' (fit for garrison duty only) while most of the officers were on six months home service after long periods of trench duty.

Hitherto the 2/10th Battalion's history had been that of a typical, if somewhat static, Home Service unit. In July, 1918, however, the British sent an expeditionary force to Murmansk. The idea was to help to precipitate the overthrow of the Bolshevik government, thought to be merely a German puppet régime, and to bring about the re-instatement of the Tsar who was believed still to have the confidence of the Russian people. Such was the shortage of manpower at the time that even 'B1' men were needed for active service. After being strengthened by drafts from other units in Ireland the 2/10th Battalion was therefore included in the expedition. By late August it had reached Archangel.

From Archangel there were two main routes south, the railway to Vologda and the River Dvina. The operations of The Royal Scots, apart from one company left in Archangel, were limited almost entirely to a 50-mile stretch of the Dvina, south of its junction with the River Vaga. The terrain was not pleasant for the land was flat and heavily afforested and the riverine area was very marshy. Movement and observation were thus severely restricted, the river providing the only easy means of progression.

In view of the nature of the terrain, the mixed force of which the 2/10th Battalion formed part and which also included marines, Russian scouts and Poles, was supported by a British monitor on the Dvina. With the aid of the monitor The Royal Scots began operations extremely successfully. They cleared the Bolsheviks out of the triangle formed by the junction of the Dvina and the Vaga, in the process defeating greatly superior forces, and then captured the villages of Chamovo, Prilutski and Korbalski, and with them several prisoners, including a staff officer and large quantities of arms, ammunition and equipment.

By now The Royal Scots had had plenty of time to assess the reactions of the local peasants. Unfortunately they proved extremely disappointing. Far from showing any desire to rise against the Bolsheviks they were utterly indifferent to the issues of the war. Though not actively hostile, no more could be expected from them than food, shelter and help in felling trees.

The negative attitude of the peasants notwithstanding, The Royal Scots continued to press southwards along the Dvina after their initial victory. The most notable feature of their advance was the capture of the strongly fortified village of Pless. A frontal attack being virtually impossible, a flanking march was attempted by 'A' Company less one platoon. The going proved extremely difficult, reducing speed to about half a mile an hour at times. The men were permanently at least ankle deep in water, and often trees had to be felled to cross the deepest pools and ditches. On drawing level with Pless the Company found its way barred by an impassable marsh and was forced to spend the night leaning against trees before setting off the next day for a mill, some eight or nine miles off, where it at last found food. The day after, Major Skeil, the CO, determining on a bold front, marched on Kurgomin, south of Pless. Fortunately the ruse worked. The Russians, believing they were opposed by a force of 8,000, evacuated both Kurgomin and Pless, thus successfully concluding a quite remarkable march by predominantly 'B1' troops.

By late September The Royal Scots, in company with a body of American troops, had reached Nijne-Toimski. This proved to be the southernmost point of their advance for it was far too strongly fortified to be taken by the light allied forces, who therefore withdrew to a defensive line. Shortly afterwards the British monitor had to leave before the Dvina froze at Archangel. The Russian gunboats consequently dominated the river and shelled the allied positions so heavily that the line had to be withdrawn further north. With the help of a Canadian Field Artillery Battery several attacks on this second line, culminating in a very determined and almost successful assault on 11 November, were beaten off, after which the line was established for the winter.

With the onset of winter and the withdrawal of the enemy gunboats The Royal Scots had a less active time. They were reinforced in late November by the company they had left in Archangel, which had since been engaged at Obozerskaya on the Vologda railway line. Thereafter, though the enemy remained fairly quiescent for the rest of the year, raids, patrols and constant training were carried out on snowshoes, skis and sledges. One serious problem was fire due to overheating in the village billets and the log and sand blockhouses in the forward areas. Fortunately the Russian peasants proved excellent firefighters.

At the beginning of 1919 the Bolsheviks resumed the offensive and there were several sharp skirmishes. The column on the Vaga was under particularly heavy pressure and consequently 'A' Company was sent to its aid. Once again the company made a magnificent march under very trying conditions. With the temperature between 40 and 60 degrees below freezing, it covered over 50 miles in 26 hours, alternately riding on and running behind sledges. Fortunately the company arrived at its objective to find that the enemy had already departed.

By now the Bolsheviks were gathering strength. Until the Dvina became navigable again they had definite artillery superiority and it was only with difficulty that the allies were holding their own. In April the 'loyalist' Russian troops on the other bank of the Dvina mutinied and in May the American troops were withdrawn. There was clearly increasingly less justification for continuing the campaign since the peasants were so apathetic and hostilities had been terminated on all other fronts. Nevertheless two more British battalions landed at Archangel in early June. Their arrival, however, freed The Royal Scots who returned by barge to Archangel and finally left Russia on the 10th.

For the 2/10th Battalion demobilization followed almost immediately on its arrival at Leith. It was by no means the last Royal Scots unit to be disbanded. Only the 2nd, 11th, 12th and 5/6th Battalions had the privilege of crossing the Rhine for quarters in Germany after the armistice, but the other Active Service battalions were billeted in Belgium, apart from the 17th Battalion which remained in the war area. The latter unit was called to Calais in January because of riots caused by the inevitably severe problems of demobilization. For The Royal Scots, however, demobilization proceeded fairly smoothly and by the end of 1919 was virtually complete.

The process of demobilization was of course hastened by the usual reaction following the conclusion of a war. In the resultant economy drive, as on previous occasions, the regimental strength was reduced. The 3rd (Special Reserve) Battalion was disbanded and only 4 territorial battalions, the 4th, 5th, 7th and 9th, were reconstituted as the second line in 1920. After doing guard duty during the 1921 coal-strike these were further reduced in 1922 when they were amalgamated as the 4th/5th (Queen's Edinburgh) Battalion and the 7th/9th (Highlanders) Battalion.

As if by way of compensation for these reductions in 1920 the Regiment had restored to it its old title and became once more 'The Royal Regiment'. Two years later the 'Royals' celebrated the opening of the memorial to those who had died in the war. This took the practical form of a club in Abercromby Place in Edinburgh to which all Royal Scots, whatever their rank or battalion, were always welcome. HRH Princess Mary had become Colonel-in-Chief of the Regiment in 1918 and it was she who, on 12 August, 1922, unveiled the memorial tablet in a moving ceremony at which over 2,000 Royal Scots were present. In addition to the club at Abercromby Place there is of course

The Royal Scots' bay in the Hall of Honour at Edinburgh Castle, while at Glencorse Depot there was built a fine ornamental gateway, to the design of J. A. McWilliam, formerly of the Edinburgh Rifles, which was officially opened by Princess Mary in 1927.

Despite the tremendous effort to which these memorials were tribute the regular Royal Scots Battalions had little respite before resuming 'peacetime' duties. In 1919 the 2nd Battalion, after being reformed at Gailes Camp in Ayrshire, was sent out to Ireland and the 'Troubles'. The Battalion suffered several casualties before leaving Ireland, unfortunately not for the last time, in 1923. Colchester, the next station, provided a peaceful contrast and the Battalion remained there until early 1926 when it moved out to Egypt.

The 1st Battalion, meanwhile, after visiting Transcaucasia, east of the Black Sea, returned to Edinburgh and reformed at Redford Barracks. It was then posted to Rangoon, not a pleasant station, and remained there until 1922 when it was transferred to the far healthier climate of Secunderabad. The next move was to Aden in 1925. Despite the extreme heat and the problems caused by being split into detachments, discipline and health remained very good and the Battalion was highly commended by the General Officer Commanding. The Aden posting lasted 14 months and in 1926 the 1st Battalion sailed for home via Suez. By that time the 2nd Battalion was in Egypt and on 30 March the two battalions met for a tremendous celebration before the 1st Battalion continued on its way.

On its arrival the 1st Battalion was stationed in Glasgow and while there had to perform guard duties and escort food convoys during the General Strike of 1926. More pleasant duties followed for in August the Battalion paraded to receive new colours from Princess Mary to replace those given by Queen Victoria exactly 50 years before. In the same year the affiliation of the Canadian Scottish Regiment with The Royal Scots was officially approved. The Canadian Scottish Regiment had originally been composed of 4 companies from different Canadian Highland Regiments which together formed the 16th Battalion of the Canadian Expeditionary Force and which had a distinguished war record that included 4 VCs. The Canadians' connection with the Royal Scots was further strengthened when in 1930 HRH Princess Mary became their Colonel-in-Chief.

The next event of major importance for The Royal Scots occurred in 1933 when the Regiment celebrated its tercentenary. By that time the 1st Battalion was stationed at Aldershot and there it paraded before His Majesty King George V who addressed the Regiment and conferred on its pipers the signal honour of the right to wear the Royal Stuart tartan. The tercentenary was also celebrated by a pageant at the Royal Tournament at Olympia and by a regimental dinner and reunion in Edinburgh.

The 2nd Battalion perforce conducted its own tercentenary celebrations in Quetta on the North-West Frontier to which it had moved in 1930 after a two year tour of duty in China. The 2nd Battalion was the first Royal Scots unit ever to be stationed on the frontier and it enjoyed four pleasant healthy years there before being transferred to Lahore. Shortly after its arrival the Battalion was called out to deal with a series of riots caused by a religious quarrel between Sikhs and Moslems. The affair caused at least one officer to query prophetically the fate of an independent India. In 1938, however, such problems ceased to be of immediate importance for in that year the 2nd Battalion was given what proved to be the most fateful posting of its history: Hong Kong.

The 1st Battalion, meanwhile, moved from Aldershot to Dover and then up to Catterick from where it travelled to London in 1937 to take part in the ceremonies at King George VI's coronation. In January of the following year it was posted to Palestine to help suppress the Arab rebellion there. Chasing the 'Oozlebart', as they were known, was not a pleasant job. It called for extreme mobility and, as with most guerrilla warfare, rarely offered the chance of a satisfactory or conclusive engagement. The Royals spent almost exactly a year at this thankless task but fortunately suffered less than sixty casualties. Although operating in detachments and not as a battalion they returned to Britain with some useful active service experience. It was to be needed before another year was out.

Chapter 9

WHEN Britain entered the war against Germany on 3 September, 1939, the 1st Battalion was at Aldershot where it had already been mobilizing for two days. By 21 September it was en route for Cherbourg as part of the British Expeditionary Force. It was, however, the only Royal Scots battalion to fight in France at this stage and through most of the war the engagements of The Royal Scots were to be marked by a distinct divergence: different battalions fighting in different places at different times.

To begin with the 1st Battalion saw very little action. It moved to Reoux and then travelled back across France to Lecelles on the Franco-Belgian frontier near Lille. There the Battalion remained for the rest of the 'phoney war' except for a fortnight at the beginning of January spent on the Maginot Line near Metz, memorable mainly for the bitter cold with the temperature dropping to as much as 40 degrees below freezing. Otherwise the chief enemy was boredom, training being limited by the necessity of manning the frontier. It was with relief that on 10 May the Battalion heard news of the invasion of Belgium and Holland and immediately advanced to its preselected position on the River Dyle at Wavre.

The Royal Scots held Wavre until the 15th. They then had to withdraw with the rest of the British line, but they had come out of their first engagement with credit. In the retreat that followed, however, both their morale and fitness were to be severely tested. After leaving Wavre they hardly stopped moving for several days. They were in constant contact with the enemy but had no idea of the state of affairs on the rest of the front outside their own section. To add to their problems their road was blocked almost solid with refugees. Vehicles were five abreast and the traffic-flow problem was so acute that General

Alexander himself was seen helping to disentangle it. Bombing was frequent and on one occasion a travelling circus was hit. Captain Bruce, the adjutant, noted in his diary, 'We have vivid recollections of three wounded elephants charging in terror through the fields. They were followed hotly by four white Liberty horses dragging the unconscious figure of a girl rider.' He went on, 'I think there was not a man in the battalion who will forget the appalling destruction amongst circus women and children.'

After the privations and frustrations of the retreat The Royal Scots were only too glad when it was halted and defensive positions taken up along the line of the Escaut Canal. The 1st Battalion was assigned to the village of Calonne where the Germans had already established a bridgehead, and there on 21 May it fought a vital holding action concluding with a determined counterattack. Losses were heavy and included Major Byam-Shaw who was killed shortly after performing a remarkable and very gallant quarter-mile run through extremely heavy fire in order to prevent men of another unit wandering straight into enemy positions. Unfortunately once again reverses elsewhere were so severe that, the following day, the Battalion was ordered to withdraw.

From Calonne the Battalion rushed to Essars, near Béthune, where they helped destroy an enemy bridgehead over the La Bassée Canal. The Germans had by now reached the coast at Boulogne and I Corps, including the Royal Scots was ordered to stand and defend the British line of retreat against this threat from the South. The 1st Battalion was in a vital position across the roads from Béthune to Merville with headquarters at the village of Le Paradis. The defences were very stretched as the Brigade had to cover a six-mile front. Nevertheless the Royals put up a desperately brave defence against overwhelming odds until, eventually, company by appallingly depleted company, they were surrounded and forced to surrender.

Apart from B Echelon, which had been ordered to the coast before the Dunkirk perimeter closed, few escaped. One who did

D

was Colonel Money who had been wounded near Le Paradis and was transported out just before it was surrounded. He left Dunkirk with a pair of hospital trousers, a blanket, glengarry, bandages and a ticket. In his own laconic words, 'A long wait on the sand, much machine-gunning from the air, then into a row boat, which capsized and put me into the water; picked up by a Yarmouth herring-trawler which was mined; in the sea for another hour, then picked up by a naval craft—and so to England.' Colonel Money bore witness to the courage of his men, 'in the spirit of the highest traditions of the Regiment', but he was not present at the Battalion's last stand. To The Royal Scots' bravery then the Germans themselves testified. Company Sergeant-Major Johnstone, together with the remnants of 'A' Company, saved by a staff officer from being shot out of hand, was told, 'Sergeant-Major, you fight like tigers'. Massacres of British prisoners were common and the Royal Scots wounded were also saved just in time from this fate, but the description given to them could have applied to the whole Battalion, 'They fought like lions and devils'.

After the virtual annihilation of the 1st Battalion in France there followed a long period during which no Royal Scots unit saw action, until, in December, 1941, the Japanese attacked Hong Kong. The 2nd Battalion had by then been stationed in Hong Kong for nearly four years. They had been very pleasant years, marred only by the loss of many experienced officers and NCOs to Europe in 1939, but training had not been neglected and the standard of marksmanship, with machine-gun as well as rifle, was particularly good. In the struggle to come this was to be one of the pitifully few factors in the Battalion's favour.

The factors adverse to The Royal Scots were too numerous to be fully listed. The chief one, in Winston Churchill's words, was that 'there is not the slightest chance of holding Hong Kong or relieving it'. The garrison was doomed, but even so the organization of the defence left much to be desired. The Royal Scots, together with two other battalions, were spread over the eleven-mile Gin Drinkers' Line on the mainland. According to the C-in-C in the Far East, Air Chief Marshal Sir Robert Brooke-Popham, 'at least two Divisions would have been required to hold the Gin Drinkers' Line properly'. The task was left to the one brigade and it was given poor artillery support, no air support, a severely limited supply of mines and very little time to lay them.

As if these problems, added to the malarial nature of the area, were not handicap enough, The Royal Scots suffered further from the belief of General Maltby, GOC China Command, that the Japanese did not make any major move at night. It was this belief that justified leaving the notorious Shing Mun Redoubt wide open to a night attack, even though General Maltby, albeit somewhat surprisingly, regarded it as 'the key to the entire defence system'. When the Japanese did attack on the night of 9 December the depleted platoon manning the redoubt could not hope to hold out where, as the Japanese testified, a company would have been barely sufficient.

Despite the weakness of their position the men in the redoubt inflicted heavy casualties on the enemy. Corporal Robertson and three others in blockhouse 401-b put up such a fight the Japanese ceased trying to storm the position and picketed it instead. Sadly, and symbolically, it was a British shell that destroyed the blockhouse on the afternoon of the following day, a day otherwise relatively quiet for The Royal Scots. The day after that, however, saw determined enemy attacks on the Golden Hill Line. This line, though not strong, was held until the evening when the Battalion was finally evacuated. It is a tribute to its resistance that the Japanese thought they were opposed by far greater numbers than in fact they were.

The Battalion now had a breathing space for the Japanese did not invade the island itself until a week later. They did, however, bomb and shell the reservoirs and cut all the services in the city of Victoria, in sharp contrast to the British failure, particularly annoying to The Royal Scots, to blow up the Kowloon oil tanks. When the Japanese did attack, on 18 December, they came via North Point, not, as General Maltby expected, from Kowloon. They were thus able to drive straight down to the vital Wong Nei Chong gap, from which The Royal Scots had earlier been transferred. With the Eastern brigade retreating southwards before them, the enemy, in the words of Mr Augustus Muir, 'thus created that dreaded situation—the splitting of a defence force in two'.

Thereafter the situation deteriorated even more. The Royal Scots were belatedly moved back to the Wong Nei Chong gap, preceded by 'A' Company which lost 80 per cent of its strength in a gallant but unsuccessful attempt to relieve the surrounded Brigade HQ. A new brigade commander was not appointed for another twenty-four hours and the resultant lack of co-ordinated command cost the Battalion dear in effort and lives. Nevertheless morale remained high, and though The Royal Scots were forced steadily westwards they remained determined, as Winston Churchill put it, that 'The enemy should be compelled to expend the utmost life and equipment.' On Christmas Day, however, the hard-pressed defenders were finally ordered to surrender. The Royal Scots had 4 officers and 98 other ranks left in action, but such was their spirit that this final order was greeted by all ranks with incredulity, and in some cases even outright suspicion.

The fall of Hong Kong of course did not end the 2nd Battalion's tribulations, but the nature of the Japanese POW camps is now too well known to require further description. Worthy of mention, however, are Privates J. Gallagher and D. Hodges, who managed to escape, and particularly Captain Douglas Ford. After organizing the smuggling of medical supplies Captain Ford was caught trying to arrange an escape. Despite brutal torture he accepted full responsibility and was condemned to death. The Japanese executed him together with two senior officers but they had been so impressed by his resolution that they made him stand in the place of honour on the right of the line. His outstanding courage was also recognized by the award of the George Cross.

For the other units of the Regiment the year following the fall of Hong Kong, 1942, was remarkably quiet, in fact almost completely devoid of active service. The 1st Battalion, after Dunkirk, was reconstituted in Yorkshire where it remained, undergoing intensive training, until the middle of 1942 when it was posted to India. The Battalion arrived at Bombay in June, the beginning of the monsoon season, and moved to Poona for further training with an emphasis on jungle warfare and amphibious operations. It was then singled out to join the 6th Independent Brigade Group with which it moved to Calcutta in December.

The 6th Brigade was part of the forces which in early 1943 attacked southwards through Arakan on the Burmese coast. In the second half of March The Royal Scots eventually came to grips with the enemy, near Donbaik on the Mayu Peninsula. There the Japanese had two bunkers, covered by artificial mounds, known as Sugar 4 and Sugar 5. These proved completely unassailable so The Royal Scots started to dig a mine. Unfortunately this had not quite been completed when the whole Brigade was rapidly pulled back because of a Japanese attack in the north which threatened to cut off all the troops on the coast. The Brigade attempted to stem the enemy advance at Indin but in the fierce and confused fighting that ensued the weight of numbers proved too great. The withdrawal, however, was extremely skilfully conducted, and with the monsoon approaching the 1st Battalion was shortly afterwards pulled out of the line. It was by now reduced to 400 men out of the 700 who had entered Burma originally and their 500 subsequent reinforcements.

After the Arakan campaign, while the monsoon put a halt to major operations on the Burmese frontier, the Battalion returned to the Bombay area and underwent some very intensive jungle warfare training. This was abruptly terminated in March, 1944. The Japanese had launched a desperate thrust against India and one of their columns had invested Kohima, important for its position on the supply route to the 14th Army. The Battalion, now part of the 4th Brigade, was rushed eastwards to help repel this threat and there fought in what Lord Mountbatten described as 'probably one of the greatest battles in history; it was in effect the Battle of Burma'.

The Battle of Kohima began for The Royal Scots near Khabvuma, about 10 miles short of Kohima. After the Japanese had been bombarded out of their positions there the Battalion made an arduous flanking march, memorable for its dampness, to a point overlooking the enemy's line of retreat. Kohima itself had by now been relieved but for The Royal Scots the battle was entering its stiffest phase. There were bitterly fought engagements on Pavilion Hill, the 'Pimple' (a formidable version of the Japanese 'hollow mound') and on a section of the Aradura Spur afterwards known as the Hill of Death. In the face of the relentless pressure the Japanese were forced into retreat and The Royal Scots, following up hard, fought another determined action at Viswema, twelve miles to the south.

After Viswema the 1st Battalion had a period free from any major action, but its duties were nonetheless extremely arduous. It was formed into a single vast fighting patrol, known as 'Scotcol', and was given the task of clearing the remaining pockets of Japanese from the area between the Kohima–Imphal road and the Chindwin river. In these operations, as throughout the campaign, the close co-operation of the Naga hillmen proved invaluable, but after a couple of months hard marching, in the middle of the monsoon, over difficult terrain, on a diet of mule and bamboo shoots, the Battalion was only too glad to return to camp at Litan Bridge. There, in November, a memorial was erected to the memory of the Royal Scots who had died in the Battle of Kohima. By the New Year the Battalion was on the move again, heading east for the Irrawaddy.

The Royal Scots crossed the Chindwin at Kalewa, the scene of General Slim's famous rearguard action, and were first engaged at Shwebo, the centre of a road and canal system. There the Battalion captured the bridge over the canal before the enemy could explode a 250 lb bomb they had placed underneath it. The Irrawaddy was the next main obstacle, but first the village of Ywathitgyi had to be captured. This task, described by Major-

General Nicholson as 'one of the most formidable Battalion tasks which my Division undertook in Burma,' was assigned exclusively to the Royal Scots. Although they felt 'strangely naked' after leaving the jungle for the Irrawaddy Plain the Royal Scots took the village in two days hard fighting. Before the end of February they had crossed the Irrawaddy.

After the Irrawaddy, progress was rapid. The villages of the plain fell with ease for by now the Japanese morale had collapsed and their resistance lacked co-ordination. The Battalion was able to walk into the important railway works at Myitnge and celebrated there the fall of Mandalay in the best billets they had had since reaching India. The subsequent clearing-up operations proved the last of the war for The Royal Scots, as they were then withdrawn to Calcutta for a refit and Rangoon had fallen by the time they were due to rejoin the line. Their service in Burma with the 'Forgotten Army' is summed up in Major-General Nicholson's words, 'They fought magnificently'.

The 1st Battalion in Burma had done much to avenge the tragic events at Hong Kong. Moreover the Regiment did not remain long without a 2nd Battalion. On 28 May, 1942, the 12th Royal Scots was disbanded and immediately reformed as the 2nd Battalion. At the time the unit was in Shetland having previously been stationed at Dreghorn in Midlothian, where it was formed and from where it moved to Aberdeenshire and then Northumberland. After the Shetland posting, which was notable for the intensity of the training, the Battalion spent the winter of '42/'43 in Caithness and then after a brief stay in St Andrews sailed for Gibraltar in April '43.

The Gibraltar posting was regrettably long and the Battalion's excellent condition on arrival inevitably suffered as a result of the restrictions on space which severely limited training. It was not in fact until July '44 that the Battalion was sent to Italy where it was to have three months much needed training before moving into the front line. General Mark Clark's Fifth Army had, however, been so denuded for the controversial landings on the Riviera that he was forced to call on all available troops in order to try and breach the Gothic Line and reach Bologna before winter. Thus it was that after barely a fortnight's training the Battalion moved north to Florence as part of the 66th Brigade in the 1st British Infantry Division.

The Division's first task was that of 'leaning against' the enemy. This involved the Battalion in constant patrolling, to test enemy strength, in the course of which some sharp minor engagements were fought, notably at Castel di Poggio and Vincigliata. The Battalion then made a brief probe up Route 65, which led directly to Bologna, before advancing up the Arrow Route, further to the East. The German positions here were immensely strong and the lines of communication so poor that the Battalion was supplied by mule train. Nevertheless when the assault on the Gothic Line began on 14 September Monte Prefetto, the 66th Brigade's objective, was captured in less than thirty-six hours. This resounding success was followed up by an attack on Monte Pratone, at the special request of General Mark Clark, in which 'C' Company in particular distinguished itself. The Royal Scots then moved on to the precipitous slopes of Monte Paganino and despite fierce resistance took the peak on 20 September. They had now reached the watershed of the Apennines.

The successful breach of the Gothic Line brought no rest for The Royal Scots. They moved north-eastwards and captured Monte Prevaligo and the stiffly defended peak of Cavalmagra, before dropping down into the village of Palazzuolo. The weather had by now broken and ever since the assault on Monte Paganino there had been almost continuous heavy rain. In addition to making conditions thoroughly uncomfortable this created supply problems. The Arrow Route remained closed and the mule train could only reach Palazzuolo over the alarming mountain road known as the Bullock Route which was frequently blocked by streams in flood. Notwithstanding these difficulties, from Palazzuolo The Royal Scots moved right round Monte Gamberaldi, which was holding up the entire Divisional advance, and by their mere presence in the rear precipitated the enemy's withdrawal from the position. There followed a much needed rest and refit (the Battalion was by now reduced to three under-strength rifle companies) and then a period of patrolling and minor actions in the Sintria valley near Monte Ceco.

It was with relief that The Royal Scots moved from the Ceco area for it was appallingly muddy and damp. Their next front was in the Monte Grande salient, first in a position overlooking the important road leading down to the Via Emilia and then further north near Monte Castellaro. Snow fell the day they arrived in the area. The supply route, known as the 'Boston Byway', was open to enemy shelling and so rough that the British vehicles persistently bogged down on it. Above all, in the words of a staff officer, 'the front line was simply one where the partially successful American offensive had happened to come to an end', and consequently the sector, 'as a position to be held for a long time in bad weather, had nearly every dis-advantage and very few compensating advantages'.

In view of their position in the particularly vulnerable hilly ground in the north The Royal Scots held their own remarkably well. After extremely heavy shelling they were forced off Monte Castellaro, managed to recapture it, but had to retire, with very heavy casualties, owing to lack of support. Otherwise The Royal Scots gave no ground at all until their withdrawal to Vallombrosa, where they spent most of December. The first week in January saw them back in the Monte Grande sector, mostly patrolling in the snow, but they were then withdrawn again and before the month was out they had embarked for Palestine.

The 2nd Battalion remained in Palestine for the rest of the war so that it was left to the Territorials to represent the Regiment in North-West Europe after D-Day. The 7th/9th Battalion had in fact been sent to France in June, 1940. It landed at St Malo, moved to Le Mans, and was then rushed back to Britain via Cherbourg without firing a shot. After defence duties round the Forth the Battalion spent almost two years on mountain warfare training in Scotland. At the time of the Normandy landings it remained near the Solway so as to give the impression that an invasion of Norway was projected. There followed a transfer to the 1st Allied Airborne Army but the last of several projected air-drops was cancelled after the Arnhem disaster so that it was as a normal infantry unit that the Battalion eventually sailed for Ostend in the middle of October.

By the time the 7th/9th Battalion reached the continent the 8th Battalion had already been in action for some months. It had been revived in August, 1939, and had also done a spell of Forth defence duties but after a transfer to the south in May, 1940, had remained in England, moving from East Anglia to Northumberland and Durham and then to Yorkshire, for almost the whole of the next four years. 6 June, 1944, D-Day, signalled the end of this long period of training and draft-finding for although the Battalion did not take part in the initial landings they had assembled in Normandy, west of Caen, less than a fortnight later.

The 8th Battalion first moved into action on 26 June when the 15th Scottish Division advanced towards the River Odon and opened up the 'Scottish Corridor'. This was so known because of the amount of Scottish blood spilt there. In the fighting at Le Haut du Bosc, and then in the attacks on Gavrus and Bougy which were described as a 'classical example of tank and infantry co-operation', The Royal Scots alone had over 400 casualties. They also saw stiff fighting further west, in the bocage country to the south of Caumont, before the enemy was routed there.

After the collapse of the German resistance in Normandy the 8th Battalion chased eastwards so fast that at one point it left 'B' Echelon 120 miles back. The Battalion rushed through Louviers, Lille and Malines and not until mid-September did it encounter serious resistance, at Aart on the Meuse-Escaut canal east of Antwerp. There The Royal Scots established 'the Gheel Bridgehead' and in some very confused actions fought superbly to hold their own against considerably superior forces who launched numerous determined counterattacks. After this notable engagement the Battalion saw one further bout of action, in appalling weather, at Fratershoef, beyond Eindhoven, before being pulled back for a well-earned rest.

The 7th/9th Battalion had meanwhile landed at Ostend and by the end of the month was moving against Flushing, the key to the Scheldt Estuary, which was regarded by the Germans as the most strongly defended position on the west coast of Europe. Although not the first unit into the town The Royal Scots met with some stiff resistance in the flooded streets. Particularly noteworthy was their assault on the Grand Hotel Britannia and capture of the entire headquarters staff including the garrison commander, Oberst Reinhardt.

Even more remarkable than The Royal Scots' achievement in Flushing was the capture of Middelburg, in the centre of Walcheren. Major Johnston was sent out with 'A' Company in amphibious vehicles on what was little more than an exploratory trip but was able to move into the centre of the town without resistance as the Germans believed he was at the head of a far stronger force. Siezing the opportunity Johnston demanded to see General Daser, commander of the German forces in the island, and promoted himself to Colonel on the spot in order to accept the General's surrender.

Even after Daser's surrender there remained problems, such as the officer known as the Mad Major with whom the General was not in communication and whom he refused to order personally to surrender on the grounds that the Major 'always shot up anyone who even whispered the word capitulation'. Moreover, until a relief force reached him over the floods, Johnston had only 150 men with which to guard over 2,000. In desperation, therefore, he called on the Dutch Resistance, which provided a further eighty helpers, and he also used the German bakers to keep the prisoners fed and consequently less restless, but he was only too glad to hand over on the arrival of the 5th HLI from the east. General Daser, however, being the first general captured by the Battalion, remained under Royal Scots guard.

After the excitement on Walcheren the 7th/9th Battalion had a period of reorganization and patrolling on the Maas near 's Hertogenbosch before moving east to the Maastricht area. Their task there was to prevent a break-out from the dangerous Heinsberg salient and a repeat of the Ardennes situation. Their orders, in Augustus Muir's words: 'Whatever happens, there must be no withdrawal.' Some stiff defensive actions were fought and it was not until January that the Battalion took the offensive again. The salient was flattened out and The Royal Scots took Heinsberg itself. There followed, in late February, a thoroughly unpleasant and unsatisfactory engagement at the medieval fortress of Kasteel Blijenbeek which proved impregnable to infantry assault and had to be bombed into defeat. By the middle of March the Battalion was poised at Xanten on the west bank of the Rhine.

When the Rhine was crossed in the north on 24 March, however, it was the 8th Battalion that represented The Royal Scots. After Fratershoef the 8th Battalion had continued to fall foul of the weather which almost upset the brilliant victory at Blerick in December, when, in another fine example of armour-infantry co-operation, the Battalion had helped destroy a dangerous threat to the Nijmegan corridor. The weather remained appalling for the attack on the Siegfried Line in January when the Battalion took Cleve and was little better in February when Goch was taken in what the 44th Brigade history describes as 'perhaps the finest performance of The Royal Scots in the war'.

Fortunately the weather had improved for the crossing of the Rhine when the 8th Battalion passed through the 7th/9th Battalion at Xanten. On the eastern bank the 8th Battalion distinguished itself in five days of continuous fighting, during much of which the left flank was wide open, but it was then pulled back and its next major action was the crossing of the Elbe near Luneburg a month later when again the 44th Brigade led the way. The attack was so successful that the Brigade reached its objectives three days ahead of schedule. Five days later the Germans surrendered.

The 7th/9th Battalion, meanwhile, had joined the 7th Armoured Division (The Desert Rats) after crossing the Rhine. The Battalion passed through the Teutoberger ridge, took Barnstorf at a run, and then, in co-operation with the armour, fought its way into the important town of Soltau. Back with the 52nd Lowland Division its last important engagement was the assault on Bremen. The initial advance proved difficult, with aerial bombs buried on the approach routes and well defended railway embankments overlooking them. Once in the city, however, The Royal Scots attained their objectives with ease. The fighting rapidly died down and they spent the last few days of the war as garrison of the city.

An account of The Royal Scots in the Second World War would not be complete without a mention of one other unit, the affiliated Canadian Scottish Regiment. The Canadians had mobilized in August, 1939, reached Scotland in September, 1941, trained in Southern England and at Grey-sur-Mer took part in the D-Day landings. After capturing the village of St Croix they were involved in stiff fighting at Putot-en-Bessin, Caen and the Falaise Gap. They had helped take Calais and then in the advance towards Antwerp had seen so much fighting in the 'polders' between the Leopold Canal and the Scheldt Estuary that they became known as the 'Water Rats'. They had then helped hold the line of the Nijmegan salient and there fought two notably successful actions at Niel and Heseler Field, although in the latter they lost an entire company. There followed the capture of Emmerich in the face of a very determined resistance before the Canadians moved northwards through Holland, reaching Groningen via Deventer and Zwolle. From Groningen the Ems Estuary was opened up and the Canadian Scottish advance across the river and down the right bank was their last operation of the war.

In practice the war had ended some months earlier for the remaining unit attached to The Royal Scots, The 130th Light Anti-Aircraft Regiment, RA (Queen's Edinburgh Royal Scots). In 1938 the 4th/5th Battalion had become a searchlight unit and as such was engaged in the first air raid of the war over the Forth in October, 1939. In 1940 it had become the 52nd Searchlight Regiment and then moved to the Borders in 1941, being converted to a light anti-aircraft unit the following year. After a period in Aberdeenshire the Regiment moved south, first to Dorset and then to 'Hell-fire Corner' on the Kent coast, so known because of the shelling from cross-channel guns. There the Regiment had a busy time, particularly in 1944 when it had first to deal with the 'little blitz' at the beginning of the year and then with flying bombs, while after D-Day the intensity of the shelling was considerably increased. With the end of the war came the reward for this fine service, for, instead of being dissolved, as most such units, it was retained as part of the permanent defences of Britain.

Chapter 10

FOR the two regular Royal Scots Battalions the period following the end of the war was remarkably busy. In India the 1st Battalion was virtually re-formed in the autumn of 1945 and before the year was out it was sent to Malaya to 'control demonstrations, riots, and banditry which seemed to have become a common occurrence during the Japanese occupation'. After a year in Malaya The Royal Scots moved to Pakistan and, being the only British infantry in Karachi, they played an important part in the independence celebrations before leaving for home in December, 1947.

The 2nd Battalion, meanwhile, had experienced a certain amount of political trouble. The last few months of the war were spent in hard training in Palestine and Syria in preparation for a return to Italy in June. The Syrians were rebelling against the French at the time and The Royal Scots found themselves in the amusing situation of being asked for protection by both sides. With the end of the war, however, they had their own problems as acts of sabotage were being committed by dissatisfied Jews and The Royal Scots were put onto guard duties and arms searches.

After the tour of duty in the Middle East the 2nd Battalion moved to Malta where they spent the first half of 1947. The next posting was Trieste where there had been trouble between Italy and Yugoslavia. While there as part of the peacekeeping force the Battalion sent a representative party back to Edinburgh in November, 1948, to receive new Colours from the Colonel-in-Chief. The occasion was particularly noteworthy because it was the last such for the Battalion. The Royal Scots were to be reduced to half their regular strength and so, after returning to Edinburgh at the end of the year, the 2nd Battalion was amalgamated with the 1st on 9 February, 1949, at a ceremony created especially for the purpose. It was the first time the

Regiment had been without a 2nd Battalion since the seventeenth century.

The first task of the amalgamated Battalion gave it plenty of time to settle down as it remained at Redford for two and a half years, training National Service recruits for the Lowland Brigade. Thereafter it took up normal line duties and in early 1951 joined the British Army on the Rhine, spending a year at Munster and a year at Berlin. The Battalion was then recalled in the spring of 1953 and was able to send a representative party to the Coronation on 2 June, before departing for Korea two days later.

In the event The Royal Scots' active service in Korea was limited to a few bursts of mortar and machine-gun fire as the ceasefire was declared two days before they were due to move into the front line. Nevertheless they remained in Korea for a year, mostly engaged on building a new defensive line behind the demilitarized zone. The following year was spent in Egypt, in the Suez garrison area, and from there, in September, 1955, they sailed for Cyprus. On the island The Royal Scots had to cover a good 600 square miles, through which there were only two good roads, and were supposed to detect smugglers as well as fighting the terrorists and underpinning the police. Inevitably they found the job both unpleasant and unsatisfactory and though praised by the Governor, Field-Marshal Sir John Harding, for their high standard of morale and discipline, they were only too glad to leave for home early the next year.

Unfortunately the Battalion's home service was prematurely terminated by the outbreak of the Suez Crisis. By the middle of November it had taken over the central area of Port Said, including Arab Town, and once again had to face the disheartening task of fighting an 'invisible' enemy. In addition to the tip and run raiders, the snipers and the grenade throwers, The Royal Scots had to control the crowds at the food distribution points; they had to clean out the drains and the sewers; and they even had to protect some UN troops from a hostile crowd, although the latter were supposed to 'protect the Allied Forces from the

Egyptians'. The Battalion spent little more than a month in Egypt but in that time it had certainly earned the warm congratulations it received from the Colonel-in-Chief and its Divisional and Brigade Commanders.

The Regimental activity since the war had not, however, been confined to the regular battalions. The 7th/9th Battalion had spent the autumn of 1945 chasing bandits in Germany. In the winter it had hunted game with which to feed the starving civilian population and had the largest 'bag' in its Corps Area: 478 deer and 3 wild boar. The following year it was disbanded, as was the 8th Battalion, but both were revived when the Territorial Army was re-formed on 1 May, 1947. The 130th Light Anti-Aircraft Regiment (the 4th/5th Battalion that was) meanwhile became the 587th Light Anti-Aircraft Regiment RA (Queen's Edinburgh Royal Scots) TA. Thus all three territorial Regiments were able to be represented when The Royal Scots Monument in Princess Street Gardens was unveiled in 1952.

There were, in fact, several memorials to the Royal Scots who died in the war. In addition to the service held in St Giles' in February, 1946, plaques were erected in The Royal Scots Club and as after the First World War the Memorial took a practical form in the shape of cottages for old Royal Scots which were built at Penicuik, Haddington and Muirhouse. The Royal Scots Monument, however, went far further than these for it was a tribute to all the Regiment's 300 and more years service for the crown. The monument was erected with the money bequeathed by Mr Campbell Smith, SSC, who had raised funds for The Royal Scots prisoners during the First World War. It was unveiled by the Princess Royal on 26 July.

The war memorials of The Royal Scots included a tribute to the Canadian Scottish Regiment and in 1948 this connection was strengthened when King George VI approved the adoption by the Canadians of the sub-title 'Princess Mary's'. The change was all the more welcome as the title was very similar to one the 16th Canadian Highlanders, as they were then known, had wanted to adopt in 1914. The link with Canada was further strengthened in 1957 when the Dominion's oldest regiment, the Royal Newfoundland Regiment (Militia), became affiliated with The Royal Scots. Another old tie had been recognized in 1950 with the affiliation of the 10th Gurkha Rifles. The Gurkhas, who could trace their history back to 1767, had sent their first pipers to The Royal Scots for training and had always followed The Royal Scots piping traditions, including wearing the Hunting Stuart tartan. At the time of the affiliation approval was also given for a change of title to the 10th Princess Mary's Own Gurkha Rifles.

With all these far-flung associations the Regiment's local ties were not forgotten. The Royal Burgh of Haddington, the old home of the 8th Battalion, had always had a special relationship with The Royal Scots because it was only four or five miles from where Sir John Hepburn was born. On 10 April, 1947, this association was enhanced when the Princess Royal accepted the Freedom of Haddington on behalf of the Regiment. The Royal Burgh of Peebles had also long had connections with the Regiment and it too conferred its freedom, on 21 August, 1954, as did the Royal Burghs of Linlithgow and Musselburgh in 1960 and 1971 respectively.

The 1st Battalion meanwhile, after the hectic moves of the early '50s, was able to spend the whole of 1957 on home service. Early the next year the Battalion returned to Berlin. Its stay there covered a period of political tension in 1959, when it looked as if there might have to be another Berlin Airlift. The only effect on The Royal Scots, however, was to prevent the entire Battalion leaving the city for training which had to be carried out by companies. Much of 1960 was spent back in Britain but before the end of the year the Battalion sailed for Benghazi in Libya. The outstanding event at Benghazi was the tremendous storms and the resultant floods in early 1961. Later the same year the Battalion transferred to Tripoli and after an uneventful stay there returned to Britain in the spring of 1963.

The Regimental Depot at this time was at Berwick where The Royal Scots had been sharing with the KOSB since 1960. They had been moved once before since the war, staying at Dreghorn, near Redford Barracks, from 1951 to 1954 while parts of Glencorse Barracks were renovated. On this second occasion Glencorse was again being renovated, but far more extensively, for it was now the headquarters of the Lowland Brigade. The formation of this Brigade, as part of the general reorganization of the Army, meant that the regimental headquarters and museum had to be transferred to Edinburgh Castle. In addition, as a symbol of the importance of Brigade integration and loyalty, the 1st Battalion had to replace its cap badge with a new Lowland Brigade badge, which it did at a ceremonial parade on 20 January, 1959. The material benefits of these changes were to be seen in May, 1964, when the Princess Royal officially opened the rebuilt Glencorse barracks as the Lowland Brigade Depot.

May, 1964, also saw the 1st Battalion put on five days notice for Aden but it was not until near the end of the year that it actually moved to the Protectorate. Aden was not a popular station at the best of times. One Royal Scot described it as 'a miasma of damp heat and dust clouds'. For the troops trying to fight the rebels in the mountainous terrain of the Radfan it was even worse. In fact the campaign was considered to be 75 per cent administrative, climatic and terrain difficulties and 25 per cent war. Movement was governed by the simple but illuminating factor of two water bottles per man per mountain. In addition to the problems posed by the country one Royal Scots detachment even had to cope with the difficulties of running a camel patrol.

The 1st Battalion fought the conditions in Aden until February, 1966, when it returned thankfully to Britain. In the meantime The Royal Scots had suffered a most grievous loss when the Princess Royal died on 28 March, 1965. She had been Colonel-in-Chief of the Regiment since just before the end of the First World War and so for almost fifty years Royal Scots of every rank had benefited from the interest she displayed in them and the 'whole-hearted devotion' she gave to them. In Augustus Muir's words, 'No regiment was more fortunate in its Colonel-in-Chief,' and her Colonelcy was fittingly commemorated by a memorial, in the form of an extension to The Royal Scots Monument, which was unveiled on 1 May, 1968 by Her Majesty the Queen.

Unfortunately the 1st Battalion was not able to be present at the unveiling ceremony for before the end of 1966 it was back in Germany. Early in the following year it heard that it was to become a mechanized battalion with the British Army of the Rhine. A welcome organizational change occurred in 1968, for the Highland and Lowland Brigades merged to form the Scottish Division, and as a result the Battalion was allowed to revert to the Royal Scots cap badge. In the same year the entire Battalion took part in an exercise in Libya and several detachments also went on training courses in Norway and Canada at around this time. The Battalion was thus particularly well prepared when in early 1970 it was selected to join the Allied Command Europe Mobile Force which had the job of defending the Northern and Southern flanks of the Continent.

In sharp contrast to the activity and recognition of the 1st Battalion during the '60s was the steady reduction of the territorial units. In 1961 the 8th and 7th/9th Battalions were amalgamated as the 8th/9th Battalion and for the first time in its history the 'Dandy Ninth' were without the kilt, only the band being allowed to continue wearing it. Far more drastic changes occurred in 1967 when the Territorial Army was disbanded and in the new TAVR The Royal Scots units were 'A' Company (The Royal Scots) 52nd (Lowland) Volunteers, Headquarters and 'A' Company The Royal Scots/Cameronians Territorials, and The Royal Scots (East Lowlands) Military Band. Further reductions followed in 1968 with the disbandment of The Royal Scots/Cameronians Territorials, but in the units that remained the best of The Royal Scots spirit and traditions continued to be upheld.

The courage and perseverance that these traditions implied was tested to the full when in March, 1970, the 1st Battalion was sent on an emergency tour of Belfast. The Battalion remained there until July and although there were only two major out-breaks of rioting and violence, at the beginning and end of the tour, the strain was constant. The Battalion had to do guard duty, conduct arms searches, destroy street barriers and maintain the peace by keeping the opposing factions apart. Moreover these tasks had to be carried out under intense provocation. Accusations of anti-Catholic bias were made, of which The Royal Scots were conclusively cleared, and the peacekeeping force was frequently subject to a hail of stones and abuse with children among the worst culprits.

In addition to the hostility of sections of the populace The Royal Scots had to deal with the guerrilla warfare of the IRA, a particularly pernicious example of the type of enemy with whom they had become only too familiar in Cyprus and Suez. Not content with sniping and sneak raiding the terrorists displayed a vicious and callous ingenuity in their use of bombs and booby traps. Bombs were left in cars, prams, suitcases and the ubiquitous brown paper parcels. As often as not their victims were innocent passers-by, but to the IRA, as on occasion to the Protestant extremists, this was no deterrent.

Unfortunately The Royal Scots had not by any means seen the last of Belfast, for after Exercise 'Hardfall' in Norway in early 1971 they had another tour of duty in Northern Ireland in June and July. There followed the multinational Exercise 'Hellenic Express' in the mountains of Macedonia during September and a further two and a half months in Belfast at the end of the year. In 1972 the pattern was repeated with Exercise 'Hardfall' in February and March and a visit to Belfast at the end of July, fortunately on this occasion for only a week.

At the beginning of 1973 The Royal Scots took part in a third Exercise 'Hardfall' in Norway. Thus, 340 years afterwards, the Regiment was still training for the continental warfare for which it had been founded in 1633. In that warfare the great reputation of The Royal Scots had been established and it has been maintained ever since. The First of Foot they were and the First of Foot they remain.

Battle Honours

TANGIER, 1680; NAMUR, 1695; BLENHEIM; RAMILLIES; OUDENARDE; MALPLAQUET; LOUISBURG; HAVANNAH; EGMONT-OP-ZEE; ST LUCIA, 1803; CORUNNA; BUSACO; SALAMANCA; VITTORIA; ST SEBASTIAN; NIVE; PENINSULA; NIAGARA; WATERLOO; NAGPORE; MAHEIDPOOR; AVA; ALMA; INKERMAN; SEVASTOPOL; TAKU FORTS; PEKIN, 1860; SOUTH AFRICA, 1899–1902.

Mons; LE CATEAU; Retreat from Mons; MARNE. 1914, '18; Aisne, 1914; La Bassée, 1914; Neuve Chapelle; YPRES, 1915, '17, '18; Gravenstafel; St Julien; Frezenberg; Bellewaarde; Aubers; Festubert, 1915; LOOS; SOMME, 1916, '18; Albert, 1916, '18; Bazentin; Pozieres; Flers-Courcelette; Le Transloy; Ancre Heights; Ancre, 1916, '18; ARRAS, 1917, '18; Scarpe, 1917, '18; Arleux; Pilckem; Langemarck, 1917; Menin Road; Polygon Wood; Poelcappelle; Passchendaele; Cambria, 1917; St Quentin; Rosières; LYS; Estaires; Messines, 1918; Hazebrouk; Bailleul; Kemmel; Béthune; Soissonais-Ourcq; Tardenois; Amiens; Bapaume, 1918; Drocourt-Queant; Hindenburg Line; Canal du Nord; St Quentin Canal; Beaurevoir; Courtrai; Selle; Sambre; France and Flanders, 1914–18; STRUMA; Macedonia, 1915–18; Helles; Landing at Helles; Krithia; Suvla; Scimitar Hill; Gallipoli, 1915–16; Rumani; Egypt, 1915–16; Gaza; El Mughar; Nebi Samwil; Jaffa; PALESTINE, 1917–18; Archangel, 1918–19.

Dyle; DEFENCE OF ESCAUT; St Omer-La Bassée; ODON; Cheux; Defence of Rauray; Caen; Esquay; Mont Pincon; AART; Nederrijn; Best; Scheldt; FLUSHING; Meijel; Venlo Pocket; Roer; Rhineland; Reichswald; Cleve; Goch; RHINE: Uelzen; Bremen; Artlenberg; NORTH-WEST EUROPE, 1940, '44–45; GOTHIC LINE: Marradi; Monte Gamberaldi; ITALY, 1944–45; South-East Asia, 1941; Donbaik; KOHIMA; Relief of Kohima; Aradura; Shwebo; Mandalay; BURMA, 1943–45.

The Battle Honours in capitals are those borne on the

Colours. There is also 'The Sphinx superscribed Egypt' which commemorates the conquest of Egypt in 1801.

The official description of the Colours is 'The Royal Cypher within the Collar of the Order of the Thistle, with the Badge appendant. In each of the four corners the Thistle within the Circle and motto of the Order, ensigned with the Imperial Crown.'

The Colours

The Scottish troops on Continental Service in the seventeenth century fought under their national flag and so it is safe to assume that from the first the Colours were roughly similar to the earliest extant description recorded in 1680. This states that they were a white Cross of St Andrew on a blue ground, with a thistle and crown in the centre circumscribed by the motto 'Nemo Me Impune Lacessit'. The first major change occurred with the Union of the Crowns in 1707 when the Cross of St Andrew was replaced by the Union Flag, the combination of the Crosses of St Andrew and St George. By that time, also, the Royal Cypher was at the centre of the Colours and the thistle and crown at the corners, from where they pointed inwards, a distinction unique to the Regiment (also unusual at this time, amongst Royal Regiments was the Union Wreath).

In 1801 this distinction was removed when wholesale alterations were ordered. The thistles in the corners were set upright and surrounded by the Circle of St Andrew, with the motto 'Nemo Me Impune Lacessit', while the collar of St Andrew replaced the Circle as the circumscription for the Royal Cypher in the centre. The Colours then needed only minor modifications to emerge in their modern style, described as 'The Royal Cypher within the Collar of the Order of the Thistle, with the badge appendant. In each of the four corners the Thistle within the Circle and motto of the Order, ensigned with the Imperial Crown.' In addition the Colours bear 'The Sphinx superscribed Egypt' to commemorate the conquest of Egypt in 1801, as well as the Regiment's other battle honours.

List of Engagements in Continental Service

From the *Historical Records of the British Army*, 1 January, 1836

Scottish Troops in French Service

1421 Battle of Bauge
1422 Capture of Avranches
1423 Battle of Crevan
1424 Verneuille
1495 Conquest of Naples
1515 Battle of Pavia
1615 Capture of Kexholm and Siege of Pleske
1620 Riga, Dunamond and Mittau
1621 Battles of Prague and Fleurus

Hepburn's Regiment in Swedish Service

1621 Capture of Selburg, Duneberg, Nidorp, and Dorpat; and Battle of Semigallia
1626 Relief of Mew
1627 Capture of Kesmark and Marienberg, and action at Dirschan
1628 Capture of Neuburg, Straberg, Dribentz, Sweitz, and Massovia
Defence of Stralsund
1629 Skirmish near Thorn
1630 Relief of Rugenwald
Blockade of Colberg
1631 Capture of Frankfort on the Oder
Landsperg
Defence of fortified camp at Werben
Battle of Leipsic
Capture of Halle, and services in Franconia

Wurtzburg, and Marienberg
Defence of Oxenford
Capture of Franckfort on the Maine
Oppenheim and Mentz
1632 Donawerth
Forcing the passage of the Lech
Capture of Augsburg
Siege of Ingoldstadt
Capture of Landshut and Munich
Relief of Weissemberg
Defence of Nurenberg
Capture of Rayn and Landsberg
Relief of Rayn
1633 Skirmish near Memingen
Capture of Kaufbeuren
Siege of Kempten
1634 Battle of Nordlingen

Hepburn's Regiment in French Service

1634 Siege of La Motte, and Relief of Heidelberg
Action near Metz
1636 Capture of Saverne
1638 Siege of St Omer
Capture of Renty, Catelet, and Hesdin
1639 Skirmish near St Nicholas
1643 Battle of Roucroy
Capture of Thienville and Turin
1644 Capture of Gravelines
1646 Courtrai and Dunkirk
1648 Battle of Lens
1649 Siege of Paris
1652 Action in the suburbs of Paris
Skirmish at Villeneuve, St George's
Capture of Bar le Duc, and Ligny
1653 Chateau Portien and Vervins
1672 Capture of Grave
1673 Maestricht

1674 Skirmishes near Heidelberg
     Battle of Molsheim
1675 Capture of Dachstein
     Defence of Treves
1676 Skirmish near Saverne
1677 Kochersberg and capture of Fribourg

Regimental March

The Regimental March is 'Dumbarton's Drums'. The name dates from the time when The Royal Scots were known as 'Dumbarton's Regiment' but the tune is much older. There is evidence to indicate that it may be that of 'The Scots March' mentioned by Pepys. If this is the case the March is older than the Regiment for 'The Scots March' was the tune of The Green Brigade throughout the Thirty Years' War.

Bibliography

Three Hundred Years. The Royal Scots (The Royal Regiment), by Colonel H. J. Simson, MC. 1933.

The Royal Scots 1914–1919, by Major John Ewing, MC. 1925.

The First of Foot, by Augustus Muir. 1961.

The Regimental Records of the Royal Scots, compiled by J. C. Leask and H. M. McCance. 1915.

Diaries: Private Douglas (Peninsula); Corporal J. B. Howden (Boer War).

Letters: Private J. Willis (Crimea).

The Thistle, The Royal Scots Magazine.